Intercepted Post

Also by Donald Nicholas

THE YOUNG ADVENTURER
MR. SECRETARY NICHOLAS

PRINCE CHARLES EDWARD STUART

From a portrait by
J. F. Parrocel

Reproduced by permission of the
DUCHESS OF ALBA

Intercepted Post

Letters written at the time of Prince
Charles Edward's descent upon the
Lowlands of Scotland, his stay in
Edinburgh, and his march to Carlisle.
August – December 1745.

EDITED BY

Donald Nicholas
M.A., F.S.A.(Scot.)

The Bodley Head
LONDON

First Published 1956

This book is copyright under the Berne Convention. Apart from any fair dealing for the purposes of private study, research criticism or review, as permitted under the Copyright Act, 1911, no portion may be reproduced by any process without written permission. Enquiry should be made to the publisher.

Made and printed in Great Britain by
WILLIAM CLOWES AND SONS LTD, LONDON AND BECCLES
for JOHN LANE, THE BODLEY HEAD LIMITED
28 Little Russell Street, London, W.C.1

For Evadne
again

FOREWORD

Some years ago, I purchased from a bookseller in Tunbridge Wells an 18th-century manuscript volume labelled *Intercepted Letters, Scotch Rebellion 1745*. The volume consisted of copies of letters—the first is dated 20 August 1745, and the last 29 December 1745—written by ordinary folk living in Scotland at that time, and they show the reactions of the unfortunate 'man in the street' during the first part of the 1745 Rising.

I lent the volume to Sir James Fergusson of Kilkerran, Keeper of the Records of Scotland, and he discovered through Captain T. T. Barnard who was doing some research among them, that the originals of all these intercepted copy letters are in the Byng Papers. Through the kindness of Lady Elizabeth Byng, I have been able to collate my copies with the originals, and except for one or two minor mistranscriptions by the 18th-century copyist, they are identical. The letters now appear, for the first time in print, in the following pages. Some of the writers were people now well-known in connection with the last Stuart Rising, such as Laurence Oliphant of Gask and Lord Strathallan, but for the most part they are written by men and women who disliked the upset in their lives.

I have tried to link the letters together with a connecting story and to ascertain who many of the correspondents were, but in the main the letters speak for themselves.

Extracts from these letters appeared in my book *The Young Adventurer*, published in 1949 by the Batsworth Press Ltd., and permission to re-publish these extracts is acknowledged.

Letters 90 to 106 were printed in the *Journal of the Stewart Society* for 1953, and permission to reprint is gratefully acknowledged. They bring the story to its tragic conclusion. They were purchased from Maggs Bros. Ltd. during the 1939–45 War and are believed to have come from the Temple Newsam Papers.

For the convenience of the general reader a skeleton diary of the principal events from 5 July 1745 to 20 September 1746 is given, and there is a short bibliography.

Through the courtesy of the Duchess of Alba one of the superb Stuart paintings of Prince Charles Edward from the Alba collection is reproduced as a frontispiece.

A BRIEF DIARY OF EVENTS FROM
5 JULY 1745 to 20 SEPTEMBER 1746

1745

5 July   Prince Charles Edward set sail for Scotland from Belleisle on board the 'Du Teillay.'

23   Landed at Eriskay. Messengers sent to Sir Alexander MacDonald of Sleat requesting assistance.

25   Landed at Borradale, Loch nan Uamh, and messages sent south to summon John Murray of Broughton, the Duke of Perth, and Cameron of Lochiel. Sir Alexander MacDonald and MacLeod of MacLeod refused to join. Despite the fact that he disagreed with the Rising without French arms and men, Lochiel, on condition that the Prince gave him security for the full value of his estate should the Rising fail, agreed to call out his clan. MacDonell of Glengarry agreed to call out his clan under his second son, Angus, and Lochgarry.

The English Government issued a proclamation offering a reward of £30,000 to any person seizing the Prince.

8 Aug.   Sir John Cope arranged to assemble an army at Stirling.

13   Lord President Forbes went to Inverness and succeeded in raising twenty companies for Loudoun's Regiment among the Highlanders.

16   Skirmish at High Bridge which resulted in the capture by MacDonald of Tiendrish of two companies of the Royal Scots.

19   *The Standard was raised at Glenfinnan.* The Highland army was joined by Lochiel and 700 Camerons and Keppoch with 300 MacDonalds. Sir John Cope left Edinburgh for Stirling.

9

20 *Aug.*	Cope reached Stirling and marched to Crieff with his army.
21	The Prince issued a counter-proclamation offering £30 for the person of George II. He heard that Cope was marching by Dalwhinnie to Fort Augustus.
26	At Invergarry, joined by Ardshiel with 260 Stewarts of Appin. The Prince heard that Cope was about to march over the Corryarrick Pass, and sent a force to secure the Pass.
27	At Aberchalder, where the army was joined by 400 Mac-Donalds of Glengarry, 120 MacDonalds of Glencoe, and some Grants of Glenmoriston.
28	The Highland army marched over the Corryarrick to Garvamore, where the Prince discovered to his chagrin that Cope, to avoid battle, had turned north for Inverness, which he reached on the 29th. MacPherson of Cluny brought in a prisoner to the Prince.
4 *Sept.*	The Prince entered Perth, where he stayed till the 10th. Here he was joined by the Duke of Perth, Lord George Murray, Lord Ogilvy, Lawrence Oliphant of Gask, Lord Strathallan, and others. Robertson of Struan brought in 200 men, and Cluny was released to go home and raise his clan.
11	Marched to Dunblane, where the Duke of Perth brought in 150 men. Cope and his army reached Aberdeen.
17	The Prince entered Edinburgh and took up his quarters in Holyroodhouse.
18	Cope reached Dunbar by sea and was joined by Gardiner's and Hamilton's Dragoons, who had run before the advance of the Highlanders on Edinburgh.
21	*Battle of Prestonpans* and defeat of Cope's forces.
22	The Prince despatched a messenger to England summoning the Jacobites there to join him.
22 *Sept. to* 1 *Nov.*	The Prince remained at Edinburgh while his army grew.
30 *Oct.*	General Wade reached Newcastle-upon-Tyne with Dutch troops recalled from Flanders.
1 *Nov.*	The army marched from Dalkeith in two columns. One under the Prince and Lord George Murray, to go to Carlisle through Lauder and Kelso, the other under the

10

1 *Nov.*	Dukes of Atholl and Perth, through Peebles and Moffat.
6	The Prince's column crossed the Tweed and reached Jedburgh.
8	Crossed the Esk into England.
9	The two columns joined up at Newtown of Rockcliff.
10	Carlisle summoned to surrender. The Prince learned that Wade was about to march from Newcastle to relieve Carlisle, and decided to meet him at Brampton.
13	Since Wade was not approaching, the siege of Carlisle was continued.
14	Price's and Ligonier's Foot, and Hamilton's and Ligonier's Dragoons arrived in Edinburgh.
15	Carlisle surrendered.
17	Wade, arriving at Hexham, and hearing that Carlisle had surrendered, returned to Newcastle.
22	The Prince at Penrith, Lord John Drummond arrived at Montrose, Stonehaven, and Peterhead with some 800 men.
27	Duke of Cumberland took command of Ligonier's army at Lichfield.
29	Reached Manchester through Kendal, Lancaster, Preston, and Wigan. It was decided to go on to Derby in the hope of an English rising.
1 *Dec.*	The Prince reached Macclesfield, where, news arriving that Cumberland was at Lichfield, it was decided to try to get between his army and London. Lord George Murray took a column to Congleton, on the road to Lichfield, which forced Cumberland to retire to Stone. Lord George then went through Leek and Ashbourne, joining the Prince on 4 December at Derby. The Prince, with the remainder of the army, went straight through Leek and Ashbourne to Derby.
4–5	The Prince at Derby. He learned that Wade was at Wetherby, Cumberland at Lichfield, and that an army was assembling on Finchley Common to defend London, and the retreat to Scotland was decided on, much against the wishes of the Prince.
6	The retreat began.
8	Cumberland left Meriden in pursuit, and reached Macclesfield on the 10th, two days after the Highland army had

8 *Dec.*	left. Wade sent his cavalry under General Oglethorpe from Wakefield on the 10th, and they joined Cumberland at Preston on the 13th, only a day behind the Prince, while Wade went back to Newcastle.
18	*The Skirmish of Clifton,* when the rearguard of the Highland army were attacked by a body of Cumberland's cavalry and dismounted dragoons. They were beaten off and Lord George made good his retreat to Penrith.
19	The Prince reached Carlisle. At a council of war it was decided to march to Scotland and join the forces assembled there. The Prince decided to leave a garrison behind at Carlisle in order to facilitate a future descent into England, which consisted of about 400 men and included the Manchester Regiment. Colonel Francis Townley was left commandant of the town, and John Hamilton governor of the castle.
20	The Highland army crossed the Esk, and divided into two columns, Lord George Murray with the Lowland Regiments going through Ecclefechan, Moffat, and Hamilton to reach Glasgow on the 25th, which the Prince reached on the 26th.
	Lord Lovat, taken prisoner by Loudoun on the 11th, escaped from Inverness and the Frazers marched under the Master of Lovat to join the Prince.
23	Lord Lewis Gordon completely routed MacLeod of MacLeod, sent by Loudoun to relieve Aberdeen, at the *Skirmish of Inverurie,* and forced him to retire across the Spey.
26	The Prince entered Glasgow.
30	Carlisle surrendered.
27 *Dec.* 1746 to 2 *Jan.*	At Glasgow, where the Highland army was considerably increased by forces which had been collected while the Prince was in England.
3 *Jan.*	The army left Glasgow in two columns, one under the Prince by Kilsyth, the other under Lord George by Cumbernauld, the intention being to join Lord John Drummond, who was marching from Perth with the army collected there, near Stirling.
4	The Prince reached Bannockburn House. At Bannockburn the Highland army was joined by reinforcements which had assembled at Perth and Dunblane.

6 Jan.	Stirling summoned to surrender. General Hawley, appointed to command in Scotland, reached Edinburgh.
8	The town of Stirling surrendered, but the castle held out.
14	Lord George, hearing that Hawley was advancing from Edinburgh, marched from Falkirk to Linlithgow, but on Hawley's approach, returned to Falkirk, joining the Prince at Bannockburn.
17	*The Battle of Falkirk*, when the defeated Government troops retired to Edinburgh.
25	Cumberland appointed to command the troops in Scotland.
28	The Prince, still continuing the siege of Stirling Castle, heard that Cumberland was about to join the Government army.
29	The Prince agreed very reluctantly, on the advice of Lord George and the chiefs, to retire to the Highlands, as the army was not fit to meet Cumberland, because of sickness and desertion.
30	Cumberland arrived in Edinburgh.
2 Feb.	At Crieff it was decided to divide the army, Lord George Murray with Lord John Drummond and the Lowland Regiments and the horse to go by Montrose and Aberdeen to Inverness, the Prince and the clans to go by the Highland road, while Lord Ogilvy's Regiment and the Farquharsons were to go by Coupar-Angus and Glen Muick to Speyside. Cumberland reached Stirling.
6	Cumberland arrived at Perth.
8	Between 4000 and 5000 Hessians arrived at Leith under Prince Frederick of Hesse and Lord Crawford.
15	Cumberland at Edinburgh, where he ordered the Hessians to Perth and Stirling, and two regiments of cavalry to Bannockburn.
16	The Prince was entertained at Moy Hall by Lady Anne Mackintosh, whose husband had joined the Government forces. Loudoun, thinking to capture the Prince, marched from Inverness with some 1500 men, and was defeated and driven back by a trick at the *Rout of Moy*.
19	The Prince at Culloden House, where he was joined by Lord George.

20 *Feb.*	Inverness Castle surrendered to the Prince, Loudoun and his force having crossed to the Black Isle on the 18th.
23	Aberdeen evacuated by the Jacobite forces.
27	Cumberland and his forces reached Aberdeen.
3 *March*	On 20 March, the Duke of Perth, having superseded Lord
13 *April*	Cromarty in command, with Glengarry, Clanranald, Appin, Glengyle, Mackinnon, and some Mackenzies, defeated Loudoun in Sutherland, and returned to Inverness, joining Lord John Drummond on the Spey. Loudoun, with Lord President Forbes and MacLeod of MacLeod, retired to Skye.

On 15 March, Lord George advanced quickly into Perthshire with his Atholmen, was joined by Cluny at Ruthven, and on the 17th he surprised thirty Government posts and took them all, and the same day he attacked Blair Castle. On 2 April, Crawford and his Hessians having reached Dunkeld, the siege of Blair Castle was abandoned, and Lord George returned to Inverness, leaving Cluny to guard the Badenoch passes. Lord John Drummond, with his headquarters at Gordon Castle, his cavalry at Cullen and Strathbogie, and his infantry at surrounding places, was defending the Spey. On 17 March, owing to the advance of General Bland, John Roy Stewart was forced to retire from Strathbogie to Keith and Forchabers. On the 20th, Major Nicholas Glascoe surprised the Government force which had occupied Keith and captured nearly the whole garrison at the *Skirmish of Keith*.

On 25 March, the 'Hazard' sloop, captured earlier by the Prince's forces and renamed 'Prince Charles,' which was returning from France with some £12,000 in money and stores, was captured. Lord Cromarty, his son Lord MacLeod, Barrisdale, Glengyle, and Mackinnon were sent to attempt its recovery, and were taken prisoners at Dunrobin Castle.

On 8 April Cumberland left Aberdeen, and concentrated his army at Cullen on the 11th, where he was joined by Albemarle. They crossed the Spey, and arrived at Nairn on the 14th. Perth and Drummond retired before them, to reach Culloden on the 14th.

15 *April*	The Prince's army marched at night towards Nairn to surprise Cumberland, whose forces were not expected to be alert as it was their commander's birthday, but they were obliged to abandon the attempt owing to various contingencies, when within three miles of Nairn.
16	*The Battle of Culloden*, when the Prince's army was totally defeated in twenty-five minutes.
20	The remains of the Prince's army, assembled at Ruthven, received a message from the Prince telling them to seek their own safety.
20 *Sept.*	After five months of wandering in the Highlands and Islands of Scotland, Prince Charles Edward Stuart embarked in the French ship 'L'Heureux' on 19 September at Borradale, Loch nan Uamh, and sailed for France in the very early morning of the 20th.

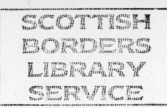
Intercepted Post

LETTER 1

Prince Charles Edward Stuart landed at Borradale on Loch nan Uamh on 5 August 1745 with a few companions, Sir John MacDonald an Irish soldier of fortune mentioned in the following letter, being one. During the next week or two he was joined by two or three of the more influential chiefs, including Donald Cameron of Lochiel, and by the time he raised his standard at Glenfinnan on 19 August where the Manifest and Commission appointing him Regent were read, he was at the head of some 1200 men.

On 16 August Captain Scott of the first Royal Scots, together with a number of his men, had been captured by MacDonald of Tendrish at High Bridge some six miles from Fort William, and the first blood in the campaign therefore went to the Prince. Ludovick Grant of Castle Grant, Morayshire, son-in-law of Lord Findlater, had declared for the Government, but Simon, Lord Lovat, cunning rascal that he was, although in correspondence with Lord President Forbes about the movements of the Highland army, sent word to the Prince by his cousin Frazer of Gortleg explaining that the reason he had not called out his clan was that he was being closely watched by the Lord President.

The first news that Sir John Cope, commander-in-chief of the Government forces in Scotland, had of the Prince's landing was on 8 August, and he at once arranged the assembling of an army at Stirling. Having strengthened the garrisons at Edinburgh, Glasgow, and Stirling, where Gardiner's Dragoons were to guard the passage over the Forth, Sir John arrived at Stirling on 19 August the day of

the raising of the Standard at Glenfinnan. The Duke of Perth joined
the Prince later at Perth on 4 September after narrowly escaping
arrest. He was James Drummond, grandson of James, 4th Earl of
Perth called Duke of Perth by the Jacobites, as he had been created
Duke by James II at St. Germain's. Such was the position when
William Smith wrote the following letter.

Sir: I take this opportunity to tell you that our news here are
various from Edinburgh, but what seems to be depended on is
that the Rebells in and about Lochaber are about 3 or 4000 men
including three Regiments of French with Cannon are under
Genl. McDonald of the Family of Antrim in Ireland, an officer
formerly in the Russian Service. They have intercepted and taken
prisoner two Companys of our Forces going to Fort William
having killed nine or ten of them in the skirmish. There is a
Manifesto likewise published, signed Charles Regent: but not
come this length, some say 3000 French besides Highlanders and
that these are composed of Irish in the French service. The above
Account we have from one who being prisoner with them two
days escaped, hath made Affidt. accordingly. They have stopp'd
all Posts, so that we can have little knowledge what they are
doing: Genl. Cope went last week from Stirling with 1000 men,
and expected to be joined by 2 or 3 Regiments, but I'm afraid
not so many neither was he joined by any when got behind
Perth, tho' then within 60 or 70 miles of the Rebells,
however it is currently reported that the Laird of Grant
has raised 1000 men and Lord Lovat 500, both which have
joined Genl. Cope so that we hope they'l be as many
Highlanders on our side as on theirs: and that before this
time some action has been between which we expect to hear
toward Saturday.

There has not been any person of note joined the Rebells, tho'
some say the Duke of Perth is with them he being gone off as
there has been warrants out against him for near two months
past. There were also seen about 14 sail of ships at Anchor by
them. It is also given out a Descent is to be made in the North of
England and another in Ireland. Whils't the man that escaped was

18

amongst them he frequently saw whom they called the Pretender's Son, I am, Sir,

Yours Willm Smith.

Dumfries 20th Augt. 1745.

Memo. Accot. of the Rebells from Dumfries.

LETTER 2

After a successful descent to the Lowlands, Prince Charles entered
Edinburgh on 17 September. Sir John Cope, thinking discretion the
better part of valour, had bolted for Inverness when he heard that
the Highland army was to march over the Corryarrick Pass, thus
leaving the way south open. Gardiner's Dragoons, said to be guard-
ing the passage over the Forth, took one look at the Highland army
now over 2000 strong, and retired in undignified haste to Linlithgow, leaving the Fords of Frew open. The only incident was when
the army was fired on as it marched by Stirling Castle. One cannon
ball fell short, another went over the Prince's head, a third smashed
a tree 'within twelve ells' of him, and a fourth landed amongst the
men forming a small crater but fortunately hurting no one.

Edinburgh was captured by Lochiel and 900 men who rushed
the Netherbow Port, opened to allow a coach to pass through, the
dragoons making with their usual speed to Dunbar and the regular
Government troops for the castle, which incidentally never surrendered to the Prince. On 20 September the Battle of Prestonpans,
or Gladsmuir, was fought, which resulted in a very decisive defeat
for the Government forces under Sir John Cope, who at the head of
the remnant of his forces beat a precipitate retreat to Berwick. It
seemed that Scotland at any rate belonged once more to the House
of Stuart, whose representative, in the person of Prince Charles,
was widely admired, as is shown by the following letter.

Dear Madam: I have the Pleasure to wish you much joy in your
New Prince, and I could wish all my heart to be sharing with you
of that Happiness which I presume to think you are in. Who
would not be transported with the Sight of such a Loving Prince,

19

and seeing him sway his Sceptre with such Power and at the same time mingled with Love even to his Usurper's Subjects and make his Enemys subdue under him and fly before him as pursued by the hand of Justice. Mrs. Heres and I was coming over on Thursday last and after we was almost ready we found it would have been inconvenient for us if my Lord had known of it, therefore was obliged not to persist. Mrs. Heres and I both would have to you e'er now but the Country being in such confusion and having hopes of seeing you soon I delayed and I hope you will forgive me for not sending you this Token which I have sent you by the Bearer, it came when my Cloaths came over, and neglected to send it over but as you know my thoughts will be a little open these present times. I hope you will be so good as pardon me for I confess my faults, for I was sure to send it over I have kept it so long, for Madam, I am not such a Whigg as you always persuaded me, for nothing could give me more pleasure than to see this Valiant Prince plac'd upon the Throne of his Ancestors: for I think as he is running the Danger he should have the Reward. Now Madam I engage myself: with you drinking his happy restoration, the thing which I have often heard you wish for, but as I am unfit for speaking on such a subject for it requires to be put in a more polite and fine stile, I end this scrole and begs you will forgive me and I ask the favour you will write me soon and your News. Mrs. Heres and Mrs. Frazer join with me in their Complemts to you and Sisters and mine to the Misses, and I am Madam in sincerity your Obedient Humble Servant,

Anne Dott.

Memo. A Copy of a letter from Mrs. Anne Dott to Mrs. Jennett Wilson at the head of Nedhereys wind Edinburgh.

LETTER 3

Lord Eglinton did not join Prince Charles. His Countess Susanna was reputedly one of the most beautiful women of the time. She had seven daughters, one of whom Margaret, married Sir Alexander

MacDonald of Sleat, who also declared for the Government after a certain amount of shilly-shallying. Lady Margaret, however, although she never actually met the Prince, helped him with her influence on many occasions during his wanderings after Culloden. Flora MacDonald is said to have been introduced into the society of Edinburgh by the Countess of Eglinton. Neither Robert Ross nor John Reid of Kilwinning appears in the lists of *The Prisoners of the '45*, edited by Sir Bruce Seton and Jean Arnot, or in Rosebery's *List of Persons concerned in the Rebellion*. There is a Robert Ross of Lord Lewis Gordon's Regiment mentioned, but his home was in Aberdeen. He is described as a 'Porter, carried arms at Culloden,' and he was eventually discharged from prison.

(See also note to Letter 30.)

Dr Father: This is to let you know that I am in good health at present, hoping to hear the same from you again, let me hear from you by the first how affairs goes in the West Country and if My Lord Eglintone be upon that honorous cause concerning prince Charles, or if he be rising any principle men in that case, or if you are to arise in his behalf yourself, for it's your Honour to dy in the Field of Battle as I hope I shall do in that good cause, for there is not a Man in this place but what is up in his behalf, and I would be glad to hear from you, but take care what you write to me or any other person especially at this juncture of time for all your letters are broke open and

I am ever more your
Loving son
Robert Ross.

Perth Octor. 12th 1745.

Memo. From Robt. Ross of Perth to John Reid of Killwining [Kilwinning].

LETTER 4

After Prestonpans the Prince settled down at Holyroodhouse to consolidate the position both of his men and his equipment. He formed a Council which met every day, consisting of the Duke of

Perth, Lord Lewis Gordon, Lord George Murray, the Lords Elcho, Ogilvy, Pitsligo and Nairn, Lochiel, Keppoch, Clanranald, Glencoe, Lochgarry, Ardshiel, Sheridan, O'Sullivan, Glenbucket, and Murray of Broughton, who acted as secretary and kept the minutes. From the first there was friction between the Irish and Scottish members, and between Lord George Murray and Murray of Broughton. This was the Council which eventually decided on the disastrous retreat from Derby.

The Castle held out, despite the fact that the Prince attempted to reduce it by stopping supplies, but it opened fire on the town and did considerable damage as will be seen later in Letter 14. During October cannon and stores sent from France were landed at Montrose and Stonehaven and became part of the Prince's artillery, some of which he was later to abandon in the mud of Shap in December. On 14 October, Jean Baptiste De Boyer, Marquis D'Eguilles, arrived from France with instructions to act with great caution. He became known, however, as the French ambassador, was with Charles till after Culloden, and surrendered himself to Cumberland at Inverness, eventually returning to France. George Lockhart of Carnwath in Lanarkshire, whose mother was a daughter of the Earl of Eglinton, was A.D.C. to the Prince. Although the *Scots Magazine* states that he was arrested and taken to Berwick, as our letter writer notes, John MacDonald, MacDonald of Borradale's brother, states in his narrative in *The Lyon in Mourning* that he escaped to France with the Duke of Perth and others on 3 May 1746. The authorities are muddled, for the Lockhart who surrendered to Cope at Berwick was George Lockhart's father. He was not allowed to return to Scotland for some time after the suppression of the Rising and was confined with his family to the boundaries of the county of York. George Lockhart, junior, was never pardoned and died at Paris in 1761.

(See also Letter 7.)

Dr B: I was favoured with yours of the 11th which had not been opened. My wife and I are extremely pleased to hear you are well and in peace. Our Army broke up their Camp and are gone into their Winter Quarters. The ship that came to Montrose brought over eighty Chests of Arms and four Chests of Money which is expected here this week. Your friend George Lochart

[Lockhart] of Carnwath was taken prisoner going into England and carried into Berwick: we have been very quiet here these ten days, their having been a cessation of arms betwixt the Prince's Army and the Castle, who got up provisions every day, they light up a bonfire every night to prevent anybody's approaching the walls and are extremely alert. Now that the Post Office send you the News papers your people at Perth need not break up your letters because they will know by them what passes here: we have a Story that one Monday a resident from the French King came to the Prince. Our friends is still at Moffat, Sir Willm Home of Blaickeden died at Plymouth so James Home gets the estate: My wife who is very well joins in her Complements to you, Mrs. Belches, Babie, Lady Hanbyres and all friends. Tell the Lady that Lille and Mrs. Ingles are gone home to her House. I would have lockt the Room of your house before this time if it had not been that the smell of the painting would not go off. If there were any passing at either Ferrys I would win over to pay a visit for a day or two. Its dangerous going about by Stirling. There is a fellow to be shot today for going up and down the country in the Prince's name and seizing horses.

Memo. Letter to Mr. Belches of Innermay to be left at Mr. Richardson Baxter's at Perth.

LETTER 5

The incident of the minister at Fordoun declaiming against the Prince mentioned in this letter is rather similar to the well-known story of the minister of West Church, Edinburgh, Mr. M'Vicar, who prayed as follows:

'O Lord bless the King thou knowes and my heart O God I mean King George, but as for this stranger who is come amongst us in hopes of an Early Crown, we desire to have nothing to do with him. Therefore O Lord God we humbly beseech thee to take him to Thyself, and instead of an Earthy Crown be pleased to give him a Crown of Glory. Amen.'

To the Prince's credit, he is reported to have said when he heard of the incident: 'I look upon the fellow as an honest fool. I do not take any notice of him.'

Dear Grisie: This is the third time I have wrote to you without either hearing from you or knowing where you are, but its very probable that the letters are seized by a sloop, and if it should be the fate of this, I pray God that the enclos'd paper may convert every one that is in the ship, which will be a great mercy to them both here and hereafter, since never a prince shew'd more humanity than his Royal Highness does, and its my surprise that any is so blind, not to see that there are a divine providence that guides and directs the Prince in everything. There are no news here but what is in the publick papers for everything is managed with so great secrecy that it's not in the power of the Prince's Enemys to do him prejudice, and for a proof of this we get in the London papers things that done and said here, which is the most confounding Lyes that ever was invented. Is it not a remarkable thing that the preacher in Fordoun cursed the Prince and Royl Family in the pulpit, that he was seized with a dead palsie that night, his name is Anderson. Not being sure whether this will come to your hand, so shall conclude with telling you that your friends here are well as your Nephew at Glasgow is, adieu dear Grisie.
Edinburgh 16 Octor. 1745.

Memo. To Lady Fergusly, very much in praise of the Young Pretender.

LETTER 6

The Prince did not leave Edinburgh for Dalkeith until 1 November, and he never came back.

Of the names mentioned in the letter following, Munro of Culcairn was for the Government, as was James Ferguson of Pitfour. Culcairn was shot in Knoydart in August 1746 while devastating the countryside with Captain Grant of Knockando of Loudoun's

Regiment, after Culloden. It is said that he was shot in mistake for Grant by the father of a Cameron whom Grant had shot shortly before.

The Robert McKay mentioned by the writer of the letter is probably the M'Kay of Cromarty's Regiment who is stated in *The Prisoners of the '45* to have been 'formerly soldier in Lord Loudon's.'

He was transported on 31 March 1747.

Lord Elibank was a friend of Murray of Broughton, but he kept out of the rising in 1745, and it was not until 1752 that the Elibank Plot was born, to seize the Royal Family and proclaim the Restoration, a plot which failed dismally.

The Duke of Newcastle was certainly deliberating as to whether he should declare for Charles in December when the Prince was at Derby, and even the King is said to have had the Royal Yacht ready to leave England at a moment's notice. Whether this panic prevailed in London as early as October, as suggested by the letter writer, is to be doubted.

The Lady Ogilvy referred to was Margaret, wife of David, Lord Ogilvy who commanded his own regiment of 200 men in the Prince's army. Lady Ogilvy was a very enthusiastic supporter of the Stuart cause, and 'witnesses declared that they saw her standing upon the Cross of Cupar with a drawn sword in her hand, while the Pretender was proclaimed by Lord Ogilvy's orders over the Mercat Cross.' She was with the army for most of the campaign, and was captured at Kilihuntly after Culloden while trying to get home. From Inverness she was taken to Edinburgh Castle, from where she escaped on 21 November 1746. After many adventures, she eventually managed to get to Holland and so to France where she joined her husband. She died in 1757.

The Master of Torpichen mentioned was Lord Sandilands' son. He was a lieutenant in Colonel Lascelles' Regiment of Foot, and he had been wounded and made prisoner at Prestonpans. With other prisoners he was billeted by the Highlanders in Colonel Gardiner's house near the battlefield; the Colonel himself had been killed in the battle, and it is on record that wine, spirits, bread, and meat were sent from Edinburgh for them. Presumably when fit enough, the Master of Torpichen was moved to Edinburgh. This is another example of how well the Prince treated his prisoners, and is in direct contradiction of the Whig statement, 'No sogers [*sic*] wound drest after the battle of Preston for 2 days.' In actual fact doctors from Edinburgh, Jacobite and Whig, came out after the battle, and attended the wounded of both sides.

Sir: I expected the Chaise back this night but I hope this will find you and sister safe at your journey's end, and now this serves to cover a foreign letter to you as also all the Pamphletts and news papers since you left the Town, except the Friday's Mercury wch I cannot get, and likewise a copy of the King's Speech which is in all the Coffee houses printed for London, but the Copy must be taken in the Coffee houses as there is not allowance given to print it here to be sold. I can give you no particular news but only as I hear the P[rin]ce goes out to Dalkeith tomorrow or Thursday and is to stay in the palace two three days, but if he returns to Edinburgh cannot get a certain account, only that Angus Mc-Donald who has been my bedfellow these two nights past in your house thinks that their men who is ordered to March out there will not return before they face Wade and there is a rumour going that the French is shipped but what is true of it shall not venture to say. The Arms etc which came to Montrose and Stonehaven in those two ships are not yet come up, which makes some people that wishes they were not doubtful if so be. I have not yet got out to see the Master of Torpichen but he continues much after one as when you left him.

I have spoke to Brown Culcairn's Groom and he's to remember him, but had he known 9 or 10 days sooner he could have pro-vided him well, but the P . . . ce has taken all of them up and his Gardner I have spoke about to Mr. Douglas, but he says that none he knows, and that could I get a lad bred at Panmure with the Gardner's recommendation he would be, only I should know if he wants one for improvement of Timber, or kitchen Ground or both.

I had the pleasure of supping and dining with Pitfour since you went away and he and Lady drank you and sister's health, and desired me to make their complements to you and her, and the reason of my being there was called by Lady Elibank anent the Bearer one Robert McKay a boy about 16 years of age who was an Ensign of Lord Loudon's Regiment, and was informed against for Treason agt the Prince and thereon put in prison and run a great risque had it not been Lady Ogilvie's interest with the P . . . ce who freely pardoned him without a Tryall on his going to Perth to the rest of the Officers. I offer my kind complements to your sister and to the Provost and I remain ever to be yours etc.

P.S. Lord Torpichen's servant tells me just now that the Master is better but after seeing him shall write you more particularly. A Gentlewoman that came from London last week assured a man of my acquaintance that the D : of Newcastle is a-missing. Edinr. 22 October 1745.

Memo. Not signed nor directed by any body.

LETTER 7

A letter to Mrs. Drummond of Logie Almond, Perthshire. Mr. Lockhart seems to have had a comfortable journey to prison in a coach.

My dear Sister: I shall not attempt anything so impossible as to tell you the joy it gave us to hear you got safe over. I hope the same good luck has attended you, and that you have got well home which we will be very impatient to hear. Indeed it was a bold stroke but blessed be God you made it out. Now my dear, I dare say you are afraid you have lost your watch, but be easie for you left it in Mr. Drummond's house, the wife brought it up to us so it shall be sent by the first sure hand. As for news you cannot expect I have heard much since you left the Town, true or false, but that Mr. Lockart of Carnwath on his way to London met a messenger coming to carry him up prisoner, so there is an officer gone in the coach with him, and twelve Dragoons riding by. Yesterday there was a woman apprehended putting in Poyson in the well of the Castle amongst the water. Make my affectionate

27

complements to my dear Logie, as my sister does to you and I am my Dr. sister

    Yours to serve you while,   Betty Leslie.
Edinr, Octor. 22 1745.

Memo. From Mrs. Leslie to the Right Honble the Lady Logie Almond at Logie Almond, Perth.

LETTER 8

The name of this James Cumming does not appear in the lists of prisoners, so presumably he was either killed after Prestonpans, which he apparently survived, 'returned to King George' or returned home.

                      Miln of Tipertie Octor. 26th 1745.
Dear Loving Son: I am very glad to hear that you are yet living and has escaped death in the midst of so great a slaughter, blessed be God for it, and that you are on the way of recovery for I received your letter the 20th of October, but before it came, I heard that ye was alive by two fishers in the Newborrough, but I marvel they being at Aberdeen and did not come to see me, but I received your letter the Monday after ye ship'd or then I had come and seen you when ye was there. But send me word what ye have a mind to do, whether you are to serve the P . . . ce Charles or remain a prisoner, or give ye be mind to return to King George or to return home. We have had fine harvest weather and fine crop, the good white meal sells at 7 pence the peck, but there is no way of gaining money in this country, there is sell for no kind of stockings.

There was a lad in this land listed and he was lying in Waterfoord in Ireland at Christmas, his name was James Sangster, write if you know where they are marched, and when you write direct to Janett Milne, at the Miln of Tipertie for George Milne is to flit.

Adieu, no more but remain,
              Your dutiful mot're till Death
                Janett Milne.

Memo. From Janett Mill of Aberdeen to James Cumming at Edinr. to know if he is to remain for Prince Charles or return to King George.

LETTER 9

The Captain Gordon of Buckie referred to in this letter was Charles Gordon, younger brother of George Gordon, seventh laird of Buckie. Alistair and Henrietta Tayler in their *Jacobites of Aberdeenshire and Banffshire in the Forty-five* suggest that Charles Gordon is the one who appears in Rosebery's *List* as 'Charles Gordon, Surgeon-apprentice, Aberdeen.' He seems to have been active in seizing horses, for in the List he is described as 'Captain, assisted in robbing Lord Sinclair of his horses near Portsoy on 7 May 1746.'

My Dearest: I beg that you wou'd do all in your power to help poor Murdoch McKrae to get his horse that was seized by one Capt Gordon brother to Buckie. If the Collonel be there I wou'd take it as the greatest favour if he cou'd assist poor Murdoch. I assure you he made me a very kind offer this morning which I'l refer leting know till Frank goes there, but as he's a poor man and has a small ffamily it's quite right to be of all the use you can him. The Pr[ovos]t read the P . . . cs declaration he cou'd find no fault with it but its being dated from our palace, as it should be from his Majesty's palace. Write me fully that I may show it to some friends. I ever am my dearest,

Yours . . . .

Inverness 26th October 1746.

Memo. From Inverness to Mr. John Steuart, Mercht. at Edinr.

LETTER 10

The writer of the following letter, Donald McIntyre, is described in *The Prisoners of the '45* as 'Quack Doctor.' Taken at Culloden, he was transported. 'Your Brother and Doctor' refers to Lochiel's brother, Doctor Archibald Cameron. He was in command of the party of Camerons who attempted to capture the barracks at Ruthven in August 1745 when the Prince was on his way south. After Culloden he left Scotland for France with the Prince in September 1746 and returned home in 1753, thinking to be free of danger. He was, however, arrested at Inversnaid and sentenced to death under the old attainder of 1746. He was executed on 7 June 1753, and buried in the chapel vault of the old Savoy Chapel, the last victim of the vengeance of George II. This passage from his last speech is striking:

> 'I thank God I was not in the least daunted at hearing the bloody sentence which my unrighteous judge pronounced with a seeming insensibility till he came to the words "But not till you are Dead," before which he made a pause, and uttering this with a particular emphasis, he stared me in the face to observe, I suppose, if I would be as much frightened at it as perhaps he would have been.'

The Kenneth MacPherson mentioned, described in the *Lists* as 'an officer in rebel service a merchant drover' of Ruthven, was liberated in May 1746. MacPherson of Cluny joined Charles in August 1745, not altogether willingly, for he was guarded until released at Perth in September and went home to raise his clan, but only when the Prince had given him security for the value of his estate. Although not present at Culloden, after the battle Cluny showed that he was not lacking in devotion, and he and his family suffered for his loyalty; he died in exile.

Donald Cameron the younger of Lochiel (his father died in France in 1748 where he had gone after the failure of the 1715 Rising) was fifty-five in 1745. He was universally respected, and if it had not been for his support there would have been no rising. He gained honour from both sides and was called 'the gentle Lochiel.' Wounded at Culloden, he met the Prince in 'Cluny's Cage,' sailed with him for France in September 1746, and obtained a regiment in the French service. This, however, he did not hold for long, for he died of inflammation of the brain on 26 October 1748.

> 'The sovereign Mandate under Death was giv'n
> And good Lochiel is now a Whig in heaven.'

Honble Sir: Your Honour was write to sometime ago by an Express sent from here to Perth, and Kenneth McPherson who had then the charge of subsisting the men was desired by me to acquaint of their situation at that time. Your Brother and Doctor recommended the three men to my care there being another man of my Employment in the place. The wounded men themselves wanted that he shou'd be also employed. Both of us were obliged to attend so constantly that he could take nothing else in hand. Both Ewen and John are now in a very good way. Your Brother had little hopes of the Former, his case being very desperate, there was forty eight splinters of bone taken out of him and a great many bones out of John. Thought proper to let your honour know the Charge of the Medicines and attendance which before this day will be ten pound sterling, and am hopefull that a little more than £12 will make a perfect cure as far as can be expected of men of their sufferings. When Cluny McPherson arrives with his men I know that Kenneth McPherson will wait on you with his Account from whom I received 20 sh sterling. Shall expect your Honour will be pleased acknowledge the receipt of these by first post. Both the men and I long much to hear from you, is all now from, Honble Sir,

Your most obedt humle Servt.
Donald McIntyre.

Ruthven Octr. 26 1745.

Memo. Letter from Donald McIntyre Surgn. at Ruthven to the Honble Donald Cameron, Laird of Locheal at Edinr.

LETTER 11

The Duke of Atholl mentioned in the following letter was William Murray, the second son of the 1st Duke of Atholl, and was born in 1689. On his elder brother's death he became Marquis of Tullibardine. He was 'out' with the Earl of Mar in 1715, and was subsequently attainted in 1716 but escaped to France. He was back in Scotland in 1719 and was at Glenshiel when the Jacobite forces were defeated. He again escaped to France, but came back with the Prince in July 1745, assuming the title of the Duke of Atholl, and taking possession of his estates. After Culloden he was arrested at

Drumakill in Dumbartonshire, and eventually confined to the Tower of London, where he died on 9 July 1746.

'Your old Friend Mr. Fleming' is probably David Fleming who is described in *The Prisoners of the '45* as Sheriff Officer, Perth. He was said to be suspected of treasonable practice and 'ran errands for the rebels and went at their desire to warn in carts and horses from the country to carry their baggage.' He was arrested early in 1746 and confined to Edinburgh Gaol, but was eventually discharged.

It seems likely that the name 'Betty Brown' is a pseudonym for the real writer of the letter. A girl would hardly write to her father about how many cannon were being taken to Edinburgh!

Dear Father: I received your letter and we are glad to hear your Family is all in Health as we are at present, but always in pain to hear how all is with you. Our Town is quiet at present. His Grace the Duke of Athole marched from this Town the 25th for Edinr. with Cannon from France and other Armes in order to make themselves Master of the Castle, and your old Friend Mr. Fleming is along with his Grace. You may tell Anna she stands a good chance for being a leger Lady since her old sweetheart is a soldier. Dr. Father you'll be so good as write the News of your Town with this Bearer. I went and paid my complements to Mr. Griffin and his Lady. Mr. Archer has his kind service to you and all the ffamily and Nelley in particular. You'l excuse the bad write being in haste. Give both our services to my Mother and accept of the same yourself: and to Nelley, Anna and Jenney. My Uncles Family is all well and has their service to you and ffamily, No more at present but rest your loving and Affectionate
Daughter, Betty Brown.

Perth Octor. 27th 1745.

P.S. The Carts ordered for the Arms and other warlike provisions were upwards of 300, there is 6 piece of Cannon on Carriages which takes four horses to draw each of them. I expect all the news of your Town with the Bearer.

Memo. From Betty Brown to her Father Laurence Brown Wigmaker at Edinr. giving him an Account of the Duke of Athol's march to Edinr. with Cannon of the Prince.

The writer of Letter 12 was Henrietta, Dowager Duchess of Gordon, her husband, Alexander the 2nd Duke, having died in 1728, and she is writing to her daughter, Lady Jean Gordon. Although she did not ostensibly support Prince Charles, yet as her husband had been 'out' in 1715 her sympathies were with him, and she used her influence with her son, Lord Lewis Gordon, to join him. The following letter, printed in A. and H. Tayler's *Jacobites in Aberdeenshire and Banff-shire in the Forty-Five*, makes an interesting 'tie-up' with the intercepted letter which was written on 20 October. The letter is to the Duke of Perth, her husband's nephew, and was taken from his baggage captured at Clifton in December 1745.

Preston Hall, nr Edinburgh.

October 17 1745.

My Lord Duke: All yr friends and I am sure yrself will doe me the justice to acknowledge I publickly declare before them all that if my son Lewis had any intention to go into the Prince's service, none would be more unwilling to dissuade him than myself. But by his discourses for what reason he knows best, he's always express'd the greatest unwillingness to engage; and your Grace well knows in these affairs the greatest part of mankind judge by the success of things (which indeed is very wrong.) But at the same time make a Parent very cautious how to advise. And another thing I took highly amiss was that when I heard the Duchess of Perth was come to my house, I thought it proper that all her relations should at least pay her the respect and civilities due to her, which when I proposed waiting on her Grace Sunday was eight days, he promised to doe. But being on the Saturday before at Mr. Hamilton's of Pancatly's house, upon a rediculous letter from sum person at Edinburgh, he changed his mind which I thought not well of. And indeed I did not aprove of the person imploy'd to bring him the Prince's letter when he had so near and so valuable a relation as yr Grace, who I daresay would have readily undertaken the trouble, as Sir William [Gordon of Park] is a light-headed proud insignificant Gordon, allways appear'd in opposition to the Family and their interest in every respect and is a poor tooll of the Lord's of Braco's who the Gordons, I mean the Honnest Gordons should ever abhor. I believe I may truly say Ld Lewis never had any friend has done so much for him as I have done, I shall be glad to meet with no worse. However I shall keep my mind to myself: and heartily wish you all and yr Grace in particular all possible success, and ever am Your grace's most affectionate faithfull humble serv.

H. Gordon.

The Dowager Duchess probably assisted Charles with money but took no other active part in the Rising, though she is said to have entertained the Prince to breakfast at Fountainhall, in East Lothian twelve miles from Edinburgh, on the roadside as he passed by her gates. But after the Rising had been suppressed she lost her pension, and despite pleas that 'parents and innocent persons' should not be made to suffer for their children's faults, it was not renewed in spite of the fact that Lord Lewis was the only one of the four brothers who fought against the Government. Possibly the letter taken from the Duke of Perth's baggage had its effect. She died in 1760.

Preston Hall Octor. 20th 1745
I have but this moment got the
enclosed pass.

Dr Jeany: You will easily believe I had very great pleasure by your last to hear of Lady Aberdeen's safe delivery of a fine Boy. As your letter was ten days old when it was to my hands I hope she is now in a very good way of recovery. Your Sister Charlot say'd to me that as my Factor Achenreth was to come South, you would take that opportunity to come when he did which I thought very right, but as he has not mention'd any such thing to me, I suppose he does not propose to set out till after Martinmas fair of Strathbogie when they usually get most money, and indeed at this time is extremely wanted as the Cash of both Banks are in the Castle of Edinburgh and not to be come at.

It will be dangerous for Lady Aberdeen's horses that come with you to travel without a protection. No doubt you heard what happen'd to Lord and Lady Saintclair both at Cullen and Aberdeen, wherefore three days ago I sent to the D: of Perth for a protection. But as he was not home I have not as yet got one, but shall send it by the first occasion after I get it, for I think truly that there will be no travelling safety without it. I write this post to

Achenreth [Achenreoth, Dumbartonshire] to acquaint him when he has done his Affairs to wait on you at Fivy [Fyvie] and in case you think that may be too long I think there is some personal service Gentleman in my Jointure lands that we use to travell about with you, is not to doubt if you write to the Duchess she will procure you one from his Grace.

I am much surprised that Lady Aberdeen at such a time as this does not get both the Scotch and English newspapers regularly for as all letters are opened on both sides we can have no other kind of intelligence. I hear from London that your Brother Adam is soon expected in England. I suppose with his Regiment. Its probable you'l see Lord —— before he returns to the South. I was very glad to hear by your last that the Duke was in a good way of recovery, it was but a very short time before that I heard he had been ill. Lady Katy and Mr. Charters lay here lately they are very well. The Duchess of Perth having been near a Month at my house at Edinbr I go seldom there but to visit them so know nothing but what's in the papers. All friends here join with me in complements to Lady Aberdeen and you and I am, Dr Jean

Your Affectionate Mother, H. Gordon.

Memo. From Lady Gordon at Preston Hall, to the Honble. Jean Gordon, Lady Aberdeen at her House at Fivy.

LETTER 13

This letter shows that the Government was beginning to wake up to the fact that the Highland army might move south. The truth is that on 19 October the Duke of Cumberland arrived in London from Flanders, and on the same date a strong force of cavalry and infantry under Marshal Wade assembled at Doncaster and arrived at Newcastle on the 29th, on its way to Scotland. On 24 October the English army recalled from Flanders began to arrive, and by the 29th some seven battalions of British and Dutch troops had landed at Newcastle and Berwick.

35

The rumours of the landing of the Duke of York and Lord John Drummond in Moidart were false. The Duke of York never came, and Lord John arrived at Montrose, Stonehaven, and Peterhead on 22 November with some 800 French troops.

Dr B: What are you all dreaming or rather fallen into a Lethargy. I have not heard one word of you this fortnight. Tell Babie in time coming to pluck out the Beam out of her own Eye. I would upon the like occasion been twitted, with the feer in the North and a friend in the South. We have been very quiet here so that I have thought of going home tomorrow or next day and would have done so last week but was taken ill on Wednesday with the Tooth-Ake which kept me from sleeping till Sunday morning and I am still confined to the House. My wife holds out pretty well. Jamie Steuart is come back to Town. Our friend Sir Peter came to London about 4 weeks ago. I with difficulty prevailed with the people in the Post Office to send you the Mercury every time it comes out. Lord Albemarle landed at Berwick on Wednesday from Flanders with 4000 five hundred foot and a fine train of Artillery. A servant of Albemarle's that was coming here from that country was apprehended and brought before the Prince and examined. He called them fifteen thousand. Genl. Wade and the rest of the Army are on their march betwixt Newcastle and Berwick, and they are all to march this way this week. Admiral Byng is come to the Road with some men of war and Transports. The Prince's army is daily exercising and more are expected this week. We had a story last week that the Duke of York, Lord John Drummond and 10,000 French had landed at Moydart where the Prince landed. This is all we hear here. My wife joins in her complements to you. Mrs. B, L. Stonbyres, Babie, Annie and all friends adieu. This comes under cover to our friend Mr. Oliphant so cause your servant to pay the postage.

Memo. Letter to John Belches of Innermay Esq. to be left at Mr. Richardson's Perth. Intercepted and sent me by Lieut. Knight. Octr. 20th, 1745.

LETTER 14

The Highland army did not leave Edinburgh until 1 November. The Dundonalds appear to have been unlucky, as there is a note in an old manuscript which reads: 'Sir Robert Morton and Lord Dundonald shot at, with a servant killed.' (See also Letter 19.)

In 1747, Lady Dundonald allowed Bishop Forbes to borrow Captain O'Neil's Journal about the Prince's wanderings after Culloden, when he was compiling his *Lyon in Mourning*, and which he included in it.

Dr. W: I came safe here on Saturday night. Tell Mrs. Adie there is no access to the Castle with safety. They have fired every night since I came home, and this morning my Lady Dundonald was coming into Town, the Castle fired killed her servant and wounded herself: so that she is very ill. By this you see the unsafety of going out that I'le no can get any protection from the Castle to him yet but as soon as I can with safety I shall go to the General and get it. I found my house all safe blessed be God. The Highland Army is not gone but is expected to go this day or tomorrow and that the English army is said to be very near, but we are certain of nothing. Tell my Cousin that her son is to go with his master, and that Mr. Ronald has advised him not to part with him, so that she may advise with herself what to do. I entreat you write, and I shall write all I can. Let me know how your Aunt and Willie is from time to time. I am yours as ever. My kind service to Mr. Adie. Let me know how he got home that night, I was much obliged to him.
Edinr. Octor. 20th 1745.

Memo. Letter to Mr. Wm. Adie mercht. in Dunfermline. Intercepted and sent me by Lieut Knight 28 Octor. 1745.

LETTER 15

The political views of the writer of the following letter are reasonably obvious.

Dr. Fr: I left my Uncle on Thursday last and came on foot to Abbotshall [Fife], with C ... L and R .... e where I had an opportunity last Sabbath of perpetuating the memory of our Dearest Lord in sitting down at his Table. I design, if the Lord will, to go home again to E ... g tomorrow or next day. I wish I may have some agreeable news from you lying there. I wrote (I think) four letters from that place and no return, I entreat therefore now you wou'd not neglect to write me immediately and send it down to Mr. Duns, as this comes from Willie's sister in a letter from her to him. Write me what news you hear of the Elector of Hanover's army, and also what is said his Highness the Prince designs to do. I wou'd be glad to know how you all now live. I beg you'l just direct to me as formerly as it comes under cover of Miss Dun's and as the Express can't stay write a few lines directly and send it down. I am Dr. Fr. yours etc. J. T.

P.S. Let me know if Jame be come home. My service to all friends.

Memo. Letter to Mr. Thomas Trotter. Mercnt. in Edinr. Octor. 29th 1745.

LETTER 16

Alexander Abernethy, to whom the following letter is addressed by his wife, is described in *The Prisoners of the '45* as a farmer and surgeon of Tipperty, Banff. He was a captain in the Duke of Perth's Regiment, and was one of the unfortunates left behind to garrison Carlisle in December 1745.

He was first arraigned in June 1746 before Lord Chief Justice Lee, and presented a petition from 'his miserable wife and four children.' He was brought up for trial in July when he pleaded guilty and asked for mercy, but he was condemned to be hanged on 30 July. He was reprieved until 18 August, till 9 September, and then for a further six weeks. He petitioned to be transported, but his petition was not allowed, and he was removed to the Marshalsea prison. His death was reported in the *Scots Magazine* of 19 January 1747, presumably in prison.

From the Memorandum to the letter it would seem that Captain Abernethy was in Moir of Stoneywood's Company, which was part of the Duke of Perth's Regiment.

Tippertie Octor the 30th 1745.

My dear Life: I am very fond to hear by Fordie that you have been well since you went away Blessed be God for it. I wrote you a full letter Monday and directed it to Stonewood's care. I have been tollerable well this while only I think very long for you, and it makes every thing dull to me when you are at such distance from me. The bairns is both well. I shall be sure to mind your advice about everything and take care of the labouring out and in as far as lyes in my power. I will let you know everything that happens here from time to time write me if I'm to cause labour the Rigs at the back of the parks of Inchdrewer or not, and if the limestone will be burnt and put on the land. My dear I beg you'l let me hear from you and how all goes on, I shall never miss an opportunity that I know of. There's no news in this country worth the while only its dull to a great many. Tell Mackie when you see him his Lady and Daughters are all well. There's nothing more occurs to me just now. I still beg you'l come home as soon as you can. All friends in this country give you their kind service, and I ever am my Dearest Life
Your affectionate wife while I breathe
Helen Abernethie.

P.S. Your son gives you his service and desires you'l send him some bonny thing. Write me give I'l direct for you as Lieuten't in Capt. Mores Company when I send it to that man at Leith. Adieu my dear.

Memo. From Helen Abernethy of Tippertie to her husband Alexr. Abernethie a Lieut in Capt. Moirs Company at Edinr. Octor. 30th 1745.

LETTER 17

Obviously from the following letter it was a hundred to one chance that a package entrusted to the mail would arrive.

My Dear Sister: This is the third time I have wrote to you and I have never got any return, which makes me most uneasy, and the more that you wrote to Mrs. Miln that you was not well in your health. God Almighty send me good Accounts of you and preserve you to do good to your Friends. Let me know if you be at Hesselhead or Edinr. I am most impatien'd to know because I cannot stir from this House till I know where to find you, and the winter is coming on and I can be no means think of staying any longer in this ffamily. I beg you show my Lady O . . . . . [Ogilvy] that I would a been up but that I did not know where you was, and if I missed you I wanted my best friend. I missed a good opportunity last week for I could a got up in Company with Lady Jean Gordon which would a been a great advantage to me. Write me what time you think the Prince will leave Edinr. God Almighty preserve you and our friends in this critical time. I earnestly beg to know where you are, whether at Edinr. or Hesselhead, for I will not be easy till I hear from you on many considerations neither can I stir for if I miss you I want my best friend. All in this family offers you their complements wondring about your not writing. I am with due regard My Dr. Sister
Your affectionate sister and most obliged humble
Servant, Anne Frazer.
Gight Octor. 30th 1745.

Memo. From Anne Frazer at Gight to Miss Betty Frazer at the Honble. Mr. Ogilvie at Edinr.

LETTER 18

This sort of thing went on during the last war when a man wanted to go into a Prohibited Area on business.

My Lord: I take the liberty to address myself to your Grace relying on that Goodness so peculiar to your Grace, and to which I have been so often indebted. Nor should I thus venture to trespass on it, but your Grace's Humanity, and my private occasions press me to it. In the sudden disorders of this Kingdom I was called from my summers task at the Western Roads near Glasgow and that so heastily I left many accounts of private concern in much confusion in that Town. As it is of large consequence to my own little Finnances the being there, your Grace's getting an order for my going to Glasgow would confer the Highest obligation on

My Lord, Your Grace's most obliged and most

Obedt. Humble Servant. Wm. Stone.

Perth. Octor. the 30th 1745.

Memo. Letter from Wm. Stone at Perth to His Grace the Duke of Perth at Edinburgh Octr. 30th 1745.

LETTER 19

'The Duchess of Perth' mentioned in the following letter was Lady Jean Gordon, sister-in-law of Henrietta, Dowager Duchess of Gordon (see Letter 12), and was the mother of both James, Duke of Perth, and Lord John Drummond. She was imprisoned with the Countess of Strathallan by Cumberland in Edinburgh Castle for nine months after the Prince's army retreated north.

'Lord John's Lady Mary' was Lady Mary Stuart, daughter of Lord Traquair, and wife of old Lord John Drummond, uncle of the Duke of Perth and Lord John Drummond. Although Traquair was well involved in Jacobite intrigue, Lord John was not interested.

'Lady Nidsdeal' was Catherine, daughter of Lord Traquair, who married William Lord Maxwell, and, but for the attainder, his father being the famous Lord Nithsdale who escaped from the Tower after the '15, 6th earl of Nithsdale. He was granted his father's estates but not his title in 1723. Although both his own family and that of his wife were active sympathisers with the Prince's cause, he was not, and was unkindly accused of cowardice. This may not be quite fair, as his reticence may quite easily have been caused by the fact that 'the most dreadful scenes of Axes, Gibbetts, and halters presented themselves to his waking and sleeping thoughts.' After all, his father had nearly lost his head, and he must have remembered the miserable days of exile. His wife, on the other hand, was a wildly enthusiastic Jacobite, and judging by the remarks in this letter, embarrassingly so. It is interesting, however, to remember that although while at Holyroodhouse Charles dined in public, generally to music, and that there was dancing afterwards, he himself never danced.

The Mrs. Murray mentioned is probably Margaret Ferguson who had married the traitor Murray of Broughton in 1738. While he was in the Tower and earning his name 'Mr. Evidence Murray', she left him and never returned. She is reputed to have been a very beautiful woman, and was devoted to the Prince and his cause.

Alexander Erskine, Earl of Kelly, of Kelly House, Carnbee, Fife, joined the Prince at Edinburgh in October 1745, and was made Colonel. On 9 October the *Caledonian Mercury* reported:

'The Right Hon. the Earl of Kellie, who after joining the Prince's standard had gone over to Fife in order to raise men to complete his regiment, is returned to camp, and brought a considerable body of men with him.'

He was present at Prestonpans, Falkirk, and Culloden. He surrendered at Kinghorn in July 1746, the day before the final date on which surrenders were accepted. He was never tried, and after three years in Edinburgh Castle, he was released in October 1749.

My dear Sister; I think it very od that you have not wrote to any of us ever since you left the Town, tho' both my wife and I wrote to you. Indeed my dear, I must say it is ill judged for you cannot but think we are impatient to know if Logie was the worse for his journey and how you both are since you got home. Now I have little to write for here the spirit of lying still prevails. The Armie is not yet marched. The Duchess of Perth is gone home but not Lord John's Lady Mary. She is still in Town, as is Lady Nidsdeal but Lord Nidsdeal is gone home again. My Lady was with us last night and said My Lord was so very bad he had got no sleep for many nights so was not able to go down to see the Prince but went further home next day. Everybody knows the reason of his sickness, it will not hide for she is visiting every day and danced in the Abby [Holyroodhouse] since he went away with the rest of the sisters, Mrs. Murray, and some other Ladys. A Gentleman desired the Prince to look at the Ladys, but he took their doing it so much amiss he gave no return, but spoke of something quite foreign to it. That ffamily is a plague to him. Do you mind in what strong terms Lady Nidsdeal exprest her Loyalty that day you and me was with her? She said she hoped My Lord would follow when he was better. I said I pityed her more that he could not go then that he was sick. He will be in good health if the P . . . ce were in St. James. Last week my Lord Dundonald coming to Town was Passing by the Castle. They shot his Horse he was riding on, and at the same time his servant was shot dead riding by him; and Locheal's ffamily coming below the Castle they shot, and a ball went in to the Coach and lodged in a woman's thigh, and Sir Robert Morton coming to Town yesterday had his Horse shot below him. They say Locheal is to be left to Govern the Town, but I shall not assert it for a truth. They lodge in the House you was in Smiths Land. Lord Kellie is as full of going along with the Prince as you saw him with meat that day in the Abbey, but they were so wise as to give him some post in Fife to keep him behind and well will he execute his Office. We had nothing but quietness in the Town on George's birthday. No window's broke. There is a vast many transports in the Road with the man of war full of Marines which they say will land at Leith to come up to Town as soon as the Army marches from this. Today the Prince and Armie is marched to Dalkeith not to return here. May Almighty God be with them. I have no more to tell you, but I am, my dear, yours to command. Edinburgh. Octr. the 30th 1745.

Memo. Letter to Lady Logie Almond at Perth from her sister at Edinburgh Octr. 30th 1745.

Laurence Oliphant, younger, of Gask, was born in 1724, son of Laurence Oliphant, the laird of Gask, and Amelia Nairne. The family had always been of Jacobite sympathy, and Laurence the elder had been 'out' in '15, while their greatest friends in the neighbourhood were Lord George Murray, and Lord Strathallan, whose house was at Machany. Young Laurence went to school at Dunfermline when he was about eight years old, and he had as school fellow his future companion-at-arms, David Lord Elcho, who was three years older. In 1741 young Laurence was described to his father:

'Your son is, I believe, the most regular young man in Edinburgh; and at the same time very thrifty and not scrub. He has been at all the public divertions, but none of them can force him to stay out after 8 o'clock.'

In 1739 his father made over all his movables to 'his only lawful son,' and the young man was boarded at Mr. Hunter's private College, Cowgate, Edinburgh. In 1743 Laurence joined the Royal Company of Archers at Edinburgh, a very Jacobite institution, and at the beginning of 1745 his uncle wrote to his father:

'Mr. Lawry and I din'd together yesterday and this day; he passes his time as he ought i.e. seeing good company in publick and in private.'

On his way south in September 1745, the Prince honoured the Laird by breakfasting at Gask House, and later when the Prince reached Edinburgh, father and son went south to join him. Young Laurence was made A.D.C., and was present at Prestonpans, of which battle he wrote an account, and at the march on England, while his father undertook the deputy governorship of Perth under Lord Strathallan.

'Young Lawry' was present at the siege of Stirling, and also the Battle of Falkirk on 17 January 1746. He finished a letter to his mother written on the night of the battle: 'I'm sleepy just now, so shall add no more.'

He was present at Culloden, as was his father, and the Prince's remark to him after the battle, set down by his wife, is a pathetic reminder of how much Charles had lost:

'P. to L. O. the 16th Aprill 1746.
No help for it. God is all powerfull, who can give us the victory another day.'

44

Father and son hid for six months in Aberdeenshire, as Mr. White and Mr. Brown, suffering much the same hardships as the Prince, so much so that 'Mr. Brown' was said to have contracted consumption. They had been attainted with forty-one others, and in November 1746 they landed in Sweden. They were exiles on the Continent for seventeen years. The estate of Gask was forfeited, but a plan was evolved for buying it back, and in 1753 it was purchased by Oliphant of Condie.

In June 1755 'Young Lawry' married at Versailles Margaret Robertson, daughter of Robertson of Struan, and in September 1756 a son was born, who was again christened Laurence. In 1762 the old laird was with Charles at Bouillon and took down his declaration that his friends 'may be assured I shall live and die in the Religion of the Church of England which I have embraced.'

In 1763, the Oliphant father and son braved the Government and came back to Scotland, where they were allowed to live in peace. The old laird died at Gask in 1767 and ' young Lawry ' in 1792.

The 'Mr. Ebenezer' mentioned in the following letter was the writer's uncle Ebenezer Oliphant, who had also been present at Prestonpans.

Dr Mama: I arrived here on Tuesday about nine at night. The Castle solemnized yesterday with three rounds of the Castle which was answered by the man of war in the harbour. Admiral Byng is laying in the Firth with four or five men of war. It is said the army marches this day. Any letters you write by the Post may be directed to Mr. Ebenezer or to Doctor White and write him to forward them. I have no news to write you. Many complements to all friends. You may let them know at Mochany [in Perthshire] that I saw my cousin in Town and delivered my commission to him, I am

Dr Mama, your most affectionate Son

Lau. Oliphant.

Edinbr. 31st October 1745.
Haloweven.

Memo. From Lauchlan [Laurence] Oliphant at Edinbr. to the Lady Gask at Gask, Perth. Octr. 31st.

The writer of this letter was the son of Ewen McLauchlan of Inversanda, which is in Argyllshire on the west side of Loch Linnhe. He is described in *The Prisoners of the '45* as a man of fifty-nine, and a husbandman. In Rosebery's *List* he is called an 'officer in the Rebel Army.' He was arrested on suspicion and was 'leading a blind man when caught.'

The letter which follows is dated 31 October, and as Dugald was arrested on 3 November, and confined to Blackness Castle on the Firth of Forth, he could not have got very far on the march south from Edinburgh, which started on 1 November. Perhaps his kindness in helping the blind man led him into Government hands. He was tried at Carlisle, and sentenced to transportation on 8 August 1746.

Edinr. 31st October 1745.

My Dear Father: I have been in East Lothian since I wrote you last, and only came in to the Town last night, and is to march this day for England which hurries me that I cannot get time to write you my mind. I send you home a brown pownie with the Lieutenant, and a very handsome gun which you'l keep for me. I send you a prayer book. I'm to leave somethings in Archd. McLauchlan's house in this Town, If I happen not to return but am no ways afraid. We hear the English Army is this side of Newcastle. Is all for want of time, but my respects to you all and am

My Dear Father,
Yours most affectionately,
Dugd McLauchlan.

Memo. Letter from Dougald McLauchlan from Edinburgh to his Father Ewen McLauchlan at Kingerloch [Kingairloch] Octr 31st 1745.

Two pleasant, chatty letters. Probably from a Muir of Caldwell.

My Dear Ladyes: If I cou'd think so small a thing a hardship in these present times, I shou'd think it a great one to be so long of hearing a word from one of your ffamily about whom I have been in great concern as there is one member in it whose motions cou'd not but make you uneasy. If this comes to you which is a great chance, I beg you'l write me immediately and enclose it to Pegie Bavely or one of our folks who will forward it to me if they can be very particular about everything and let me know all that has happen'd you there three months a much longer time than I imagined to have been in this country. Who could have suspected when we came here what has since happen'd. I never thought to have seen poor Scotland a scene of war and bloodshed in our days. I pity your Mama extremely I'm afraid her concern will affect her health for I'm sure she will be laying this all very much to heart. Let me know particularly both about her and your B. as also if any of your uncles be with the Army or Sandy Dunlop. I can write no news from this we are very quiet here tho' between Dundee and Perth in both which places there is a Governour placed by the Prince, in spite of which the inhabitants was so loyal as to keep the Birthday. They say there was a scuffle in Perth about it and some people killed but it is not certain. I'm glad Lord G. [probably the Earl of Glasgow] is at Aix. I hear Mr. Boyle is in the west country. Let me know if he is with you and if he is to be in Scotland all winter. O for the happy times we have seen! May a Good God soon put an end to those disorders and restore our former tranquility. My Dears adieu. May happiness and Good Fortune ever attend you. My kind complemts and best wishes to you all, Meg and Bess, joins as also Mr. Cr.
November 1st 1745.

Memo. To Miss Muire at Glenderston near Glasgow Novr. 1st 1745. Sign'd by nobody.

My Dr Peggie: We had yours last week which was very acceptable. It is all we can get of our friends at present and no small comfort it is in our situation who are always so much afraid of what may happen and at the same time so ignorant. We are much surprised your folk know so little of one another and I think in times of publick calamity friends shou'd be much with their endeavours to soften the present Evil and alleviate the fears for the future as much as possible. Ah, Peggie, what think you will become of all this? Our present prospect is extremely dismal—to be sure there must be a date of bloodshed and probably at the very gates of Edinr. War at any rate is terrible but a civil war a hundred times more so than any other. I'm glad to hear Lord G. is still beyond seas. Write me if Colonel Muir or Sandy be in the Army, that is coming down or Sandie Dunlop. I hope Roby Elliot is still in France. We hear the Highland army intends to march southward. I sincerely wish it may be so that the scene of Action may be a little removed. Let me know what your papa is doing all this time, I dare say he will have a very sore heart. I'm sorry for the domestick change it has occasioned you, but I hope it shall not continue. Write me of the Kelburn family. I hear Patie is in Scotland. Dear Pegie adieu, I am going next week to Caldwell if you can forward it, I beg you will.

Novemr. 1st.

Memo. To Miss Barclay at Edinburgh, signed no body. Novr. 1st.

LETTERS 24 AND 25

The Prince's 'first demand on Glasgow,' here mentioned, was sent from Leckie House on 13 September 1745, during the march to Edinburgh. It was sent to Provost Andrew Cochrane, and demanded a contribution of £15,000 together with the surrender of all arms.

Soon after the Battle of Prestonpans John Hay of Restalrig, Writer to the Signet, was sent by the Prince from Edinburgh to obtain the £15,000. He eventually compromised by accepting £5,000 in cash and £500 in goods.

Before Charles left Edinburgh he appointed David Fotheringham Governor of Dundee. He is described as a merchant in Rosebery's *List*, where it is stated that he escaped in May 1746 with Lord Ogilvy in a ship to Bergen, but that he was a prisoner. His name appears on the list of prisoners aboard the 'Pamela' on 9 August, but not on 11 September 1746. Between those dates he must have escaped, for, in *The Lyon in Mourning*, Bishop Forbes writes that one Duncan Cameron accompanied 'Mrs Fotheringham who was going over to France to her husband, late governor of Dundee.' She had a pass to Holland for herself, her child and two servants, and Duncan went with her as servant. They sailed from Leith Roads in the 'Sibbald' on 19 June 1747. This letter is signed, for some reason, with the ordinary legal phrase 'Eodem Die.'

Dear Jacob: I find by a letter from you to Brother Charly of the 23d ulto, that you have wrote me several times lately but none of them have come to hand. The last I received contain'd an Account of the P . . . . . s first demand on Glasgow, and the great apprehensions your folks were under. I own myself much to blame in not answering that sooner but as all letters are all open'd at the Post Office just now, and as its not very safe to write news I thought it scarcely worth the while. Brother Charles wrote you about a fortnight ago with the Curriers in which he took notice of all the persons that have gone from this part of the country upon the present Expedition. Since that time there is none gone nor any thing new scarce except Mr. D . . . d [David] F . . . . m [Fotheringham] made Governor of D . . . . e [Dundee] but has no party to support him in that Authority. I am extremely sorry to hear how much your trade has suffered in the present Juncture. My black Galloway is gone to the Camp and my servt Will is coachman to the P . . . . e. All friends here and in D . . . . e except Mrs. Duncan's youngest bairns who have the small pox and the two youngest very bad. As Charles is to write you an answer to your letter below, I shall put an end to this with making all the Ladies complements to you and remain, Dr Jacob

                         Yours sincerely, Eodem Die.

M . . . . . n Novr. 1st 1745.

Memo. From Eodem Die of M . . . . . n as likewise the following from his brother to Mr. James Crawford Mercht in Glasgow. Novr. 1st 1745.

Dear T: I receiv'd yours and wou'd have wrote you by the carriers had they not gone before this letter was brought out. You desire me to write you what remarkable has happen'd since I wrote you last and besides what Hary has wrote you. I don't remember of any else that's worth mentioning. As for private news amidst this General confusion, you may depend upon this that Mr. Tyler about 2 or 3 weeks ago was married to Miss Anny Craig a very Pritty woman with £600 ster of Portion. That Mr. Imrie is this night married to Miss Young in St. Andrews, Ninian Young's daughter a very fine lady with £2000 ster of portion and that Tuesday next Miss Jenny Rodgers our neighbour is to be married to Mr. Marr of Murrays who besides his stipend which is very good has no less two other pritty considerable estates. This I think lays the like obligation on your Gentleman in Glasgow to do something for our poor ladys in this country. I am, Dr Sir,

Yours sincerely
Eodem Die.

LETTER 26

An interesting letter. Charles Crawford seems to have been a man of philanthropic disposition.

Dr David: I have a great inclination to know if you survive these troubles in which I presume you have had your share. However I don't imagine you have dyed throu fear as I have better knowledge of your courage which no doubt would prompt you to be the most forward among the volunteers. Dr Davie I wou'd certainly have wrote long before this time, but as you may imagine, we have been this long time in a continual Alarm, what with Horse stealing and other ways, and as it realy never came in my head or just now so you'l excuse me. I dare say you envy my situation very much, and to tell the truth I am as happy if not happier than I ought to be in this universall calamity, the effect whereof we have felt as little here as anywhere, and I don't know how to account for it. But I am now in a manner quite at ease since Edinr. is now out of the apprehension of a sudden destruction, tho I think at the same time its the Duty of everyone that would be call'd a thinking man to consider what the effects of this will be, and so take their measures accordingly, as I imagine just now that a great many dont see so far in this affair as they do in other things of less importance. I cant help amongst other things to be much affected with the Case of our Poor Brethren, as I have not heard such an universal joining as might be expected amongst the most of them. Dont imagine by this that I am either Whig or Torie as I think the only real Title to a Crown with respect to subjects is Possession. I dare say there is some of my acquaintances that have joined the P . . . ce so if you wou'd give me account of them together with any thing else that occurs to you upon the subject as also any news you have, as we expect a Batle here in a fortnight, you'l continue the many obligations I am under to you. I design to pass the Winter mostly in the country where I dont design to be idle, as I was much behind in the knowledge of books. I likewise design to learn French and the German Flute both which my brother is to teach me. I wou'd not have wrote you so long a letter if I had not thought you would be at least quite idle, if not doing ill.

I am sincerely, Dr Davie
Your Humble servant
Charles Crawfoord.

Menorgan Novr. 1st 1745.

P.S. Must still be your Dr as I have not an opportunity from this place to you.

Memo. From Charles Crawfoord of Manorgan to Mr. David Russell, Writes in Edinbr. Nov 1st 1745.

LETTER 27

On 30 October the Council had met at Holyroodhouse to decide the course of the campaign. The Prince was for marching on Newcastle to attack Wade, who had arrived there the day before with tired troops. But Lord George Murray and the Highland chiefs advised an advance on Carlisle, thus avoiding a battle until either the English and Welsh Jacobites had time to come in, or assistance had arrived from France. No decision was reached but on 31 October, although he still believed his to be the correct course, Charles agreed to accept Lord George's advice. The army was divided into two columns, and one, under the Dukes of Atholl and Perth was to march through Peebles and Moffat, while the other, under the Prince and Lord George Murray, was to go by Kelso and Lauder, thus appearing to threaten Wade at Newcastle. The two columns eventually met at Newtown of Rockcliff in Cumberland.

November 1st 1745

Dear Ladys: We had Jeaney's just now and are glad to hear you are all well. I shall pity you extremely if there is another Battle in your neighbourhood, tho I do not believe you suffer a great deal more than we do here thro' anxiety for you at a distance uncertainty about what is passing, and terror for the worst. The English Army is not I believe so near as you imagine it, at least we hear it cannot be with you before these ten days as yet. I wish some good genius for Scotland wou'd put into the Prince's head to meet them, it was said here he intended it. I am sorry for Mr. B but as time goes at present I think he will be well of if he makes no greater loss. Mr Cr. wrote you last week not to purchase any horses for him till times grow better. I repeat it in case it do not come to hand. I write you the beginning of the week, we expected Meg the middle of it, but they have kept her till Monday, the Captain comes with her. The Lady is very well again. Mary's letter you mention, and all you have yet wrote have come to hand. We wrote Peggie B. and had an answer from her where she makes the same complaints of you, you do of her. I wish you were in a different way, if any body speaks of our staying so long here be sure and tell we wait N's coming and that we wrote three several times about it the end of last month. Indeed we expected her so certainly with Lady Ingenish [?] that when we made a jaunt to Dunmure about that time, we ordered Maters, so as to have gone from that streight home without returning here. We have a reason for desiring this which you shall know at meeting. Bets is going to Dundee tomorrow to stay all night with Mrs. Duncan whose three youngest children has the small pox. Sandy is recovering, Jamie is thought dying and Jack is very ill. The Birthday [King George's] was kept at Dundee with great solemnity, and it was even kept at Perth in spite of the H . . . . rs [Highlanders]. Service to all friends. I'm glad Jamie B. is so well. I fear Jeany L. has taken an ill time to change her principles, let us know if she is still decreasing. I wish you had wrote what Nany Mure said. Write me if W. has gone to P. We thought the H . . . . army had been at Dalkeith.

Memo. To Miss Elphinston at Bowlingreen near Leith. Novr. 1st 1745, dated no where, nor sign'd by any body.

LETTERS 28 AND 29

Lord Strathallan, with Oliphant of Gask senior as his lieutenant, was appointed Governor of Perth towards the end of October. By the time the Prince arrived in Glasgow in January 1746 after the retreat from Derby, considerable numbers of men including a force of some 800 French under Lord John Drummond, Perth's brother, and stores had been assembled, both at Perth and Dunblane. The French arms and ammunition here referred to presumably formed part of this reinforcement.

The writer of Letters 28 and 29 was probably the Arbuthnot, a Jacobite emissary, who, as mentioned by W. B. Blaikie in his *Itinerary of Prince Charles Edward Stuart*, is said to have accompanied the stores from France and saw them to Perth. His name does not appear on any of the lists of prisoners, so presumably he managed to get back to France. He was obviously a gentleman of some importance and influence.

Lord John Drummond with his force of some 800 landed at Montrose, Stonehaven, and Peterhead on 22 November 1745. Two of his transports had been captured by English cruisers on the way over, and his force consisted of his own regiment of Royal Scots, and a detachment of 50 men from each of the six Irish regiments under Brigadier Stapleton.

See also postscript to Letter 30.

Of the gentlemen mentioned as 'Super Cargoes' and passengers in Letter 29, there is no reference to any Flyn in *The Prisoners of the '45*. Thomas Goold, a lieutenant in Berwick's Regiment, was discharged, presumably because he was a French subject, and returned to France. Patrick Byrn, a lieutenant in Bulkeley's French Service, and Gabriel Fox, a lieutenant in Dillon's Foreign Service who was taken at Culloden, were pardoned on condition of perpetual banishment.

John Erskine, described as a merchant apprentice of Montrose, has the following paragraph about him in Rosebery's *List*:

> 'Commanded a company in the Rebel Army. Received and conveyed the French Arms to the Rebel Army, for which purpose harassed the Country for Horses and Carts, he was at the Skirmish of Inverury and affair at Falkirk and went North with the Rebels.'

His eventual fate is unknown.

David Ferriers, described as a merchant of Brechin, has this about him in Rosebery's *List* (his name is written 'fferrier'):

> 'Acted as Deput Governor of the Town of Brechin, practiced the highest Tyrrany over the loyal subjects of the Government in every shape; and particularly extorted men, money, Horses and Arms throughout the whole country; levyed His Majesty's Excise and gave his own Receipts for same: was the principal person who promoted and carried on the affair of taking the Hazard Sloop in which some of the crew were killed and wounded and the rest made Prisoners, and treated by him in so barbarous a manner as that they must in all probability have perished had it not been for the assistance they received from the friends of the Government in Montrose, Brechin and elsewhere. He also bore Arms in Ld Ogilvie's Regiment, recruited and forced out no less than two Company's of Rebel militia; was present at the skirmish of Inverury as Captain of one of the said Companys; Burned the Customhouse Boat at Aberdeen; received and conveyed the French Arms and Ammunition, for which purpose he harrassed and oppressed the whole country in pressing their Horses and Carts. He joined the main body of the Rebels with his Company at Stirling

accompanyed them to Inverness from whence he returned to Inveresk, raised a great many of the inhabitants there with a Design to force back Rebel Runnaways, and make well affected people prisoners, and marched with the said Gleneske to Cortachie in order to force a Garrison of the King's Troops lying there. These facts are well known to everybody in these places of the Country.'

He is stated to be 'supposed to be lurking amongst the neighbouring Hills.' What happened to him afterwards is not known, but he must have been a most useful adherent to the Prince.

Scraps of a letter from James Carnegy Arbuthnott from Montrose. Octor. 30th 1745.

I have presumed—with to give you the good—Arrival—French ship from Dunkirk—Arms and Ammunition. She came into this Harbour today at one of the clock afternoon and will be unloaded and all her cargo carried as far as Brechin this Night and so to proceed to Perth. There is only four people of any fashion on board two of which belong to the Cargo, the other two are passengers. I wish you would send a General order in case you are expecting any more. I have wrote to Lord Ogilvie—was—powers to me to Ac . . . . so—ward that the P . . . ce—not suffer. I shall further presume to—there is a great deal of money to be raised—the estates of Panmure and South Esque if they can be proper hands got to manage them. I beg you'l excuse this Trouble from one who assures you wishes both you and the Cause very well, I am with Great Esteem and Regard, Sir, your Humble Servant,

James Carnegy Arbuthnot.
Montrose Octor. 30th 1745.

James Carnegy Arbuthnott to Lord Ogilvie (tore to pieces) from Montrose October 30th 1745.

My Lord: I have the pleasure to advise you of a French ship from Dunkirk with Arms and Ammunition being landed here. She got into this Harbour this day at one o'clock afternoon, and is just now busy unloading. All the cargo will be at Brechin this night. There is only four Gentlemen, two of which I take to be Super

Cargoes. Their names are Mr. Flyn and Mr. Goold. The other two are passengers viz. Capt. Byrn and Mr. Fox. This is all the News and they tell that the Lord Jno Drummond's Regiment, and the whole Irish Brigade were to embark two days after they came off. We do all we can to raise your Low Country Battalion, and for that and many other reasons I expect you will procure full powers for me to call for any Publick money and in the General such powers as can enable me to act in Default of others. I beg you will not neglect it, as there is great loss to the Prince's interest by Peoples inactivity and for my own part I know no Body but the Two Collectors of Customs and Excise, and Mr. Falkingham [Fotheringham] at Dundee that have meddled since you left the Country. I am in very great haste, My Lord, your most Humble Servant.

Montrose Octor. 30th 1745. James Carnegy Arbuthnot.

P.S. I am importuned to solicit you in favour of Capt. Jno Cokran of Murray's Regiment and one of the Prisoners at Perth, an old and infirm man, that you would procure order from his R . . . . H . . . . the Power to allow him to come and live with his lady who is here and is in such a tender way that she cannot go to him, and the poor man is unable to support the Burthen of keeping two ffamilies. I am assured that whatever Conditions are imposed he will religiously observe. As it is represented an Act of Charity's I am hopefull it will weigh with you, and I must confess its my only motive in writing to you as I know nothing about the Gentleman myself. Send your orders with respect to David Ferriers and Jno Erskin's march up to the Army. They are very usefull here, and if called away must direct how they are to be supplyed.

Pray suggest to some proper Person that there is a parcel of as good men to be raised in the Country of Merns [Kincardineshire] as can be seen any where, and that they should not omit raising them with all speed.

Sir Alexander MacDonald of Sleat was the 7th baronet. Although Murray of Broughton in his *Memorials* quite definitely states that Sir Alexander promised support to the Rising, an assertion which finds credulity in family tradition, when the Prince actually landed he refused assistance and took the Government side. Murray's actual words are as follows:

'I must therefor do Sr Alexr McDonald the justice to say that the winter preceeding the Chevalier's landing when a letter was conveyed to him from him desiring his assistance in his intended expedition he denyed making any possitive promise but said how soon he saw a well concerted scheme he would readyly not only to join him himself but endeavour to procure the assistance of as many of his neighbours as he could, and I can say with certainty that from that time he came under no further engagements; att the same time that I do him this justice, I hope the world will not from thence infer that I in the smallest degree approve of his future behaviour. I should be sorry to have so bad an opinion of mankind as to think any of them cappable of attempting an apologie for him.'

Sir Alexander died aged thirty-six on 23 November 1746.

The Mackintosh contingent here mentioned was probably part of the contingent being raised by Lady Anne Mackintosh, whose husband was serving under the Government. She and some 800 Mackintoshes eventually joined the main Highland army at Bannockburn in January 1746.

Directed to the Right Honble. The Lady Ogilvie.

Pieces of a Letter from —— Directed to the Right Honble Lady Franc Stuart to be left at Mr. Trail's Shop, Bookseller in the Parliament Close, Edinburgh.

My Dearest Fanny: I am safely arrived here in good health and as I never will omit any opportunity of letting you hear from me, I embrace this that may tell you the news. Last night being His Majesty's Birthday many of the Loyal Citizens got drunk, and by way of merryment as there is no guard left here, they fell a firing upon some few of the Towns people who were in the Town house and unfortunately killed a poor French Gentleman who came in one of the Ships, and who had been left here upon

Account of his Health. All now is very quiet as there is a Guard of 77 Highlanders come to Town. I saw a Gentleman this morning left 224 McIntoshes at Dunkall [Dunkeld]. They say there are more of them coming up. The Laird of Logy Almond's Factor spoke to me as I came to Town and inform'd me that a Gentleman had passed this day at his House who told him that Sir Alexr McDonald with a great many of his men, were in the Braes of Bagenough [Badenoch], but this I give little credit to as it comes thro' so many Hands. What is to be more certain is that there are French Ships come to Montrose, but what they have on board is not known. According to the Establish'd Rule laid down that good intelligence is a bad thing and that secrecy is much to be commended. I have given you all the news I have here, and have no more to add but my sincerest Prayers for your recovery and Happiness, my Dear Fanny, remember that my life and Happiness is bound up in yours, and that if you do not take care of yourself now that you are so low in Body, you will run a great Risque, and then what will become of our poor little Body, and what will become of me? I have got a very good Companion for my journey which makes up quite well for the want of my Servant. When after this you see a mark like this X at any of my letters you may hold them to the fire, and now my Dearest life a Dieu.

Perth Octor. 31st.

P.S. Since writing an account is come from Montrose, there is but one ship landed, the other that was seen was a Man of War in Chace of her. She left Dunkirk 12 Days ago, at which time Lord John Drummond's Regiment was Embark'd for Scotland and 10,000 with the Duke of Ormond and Lord Marshall were ready to Embark for England, and so my Dearest Dear Body farewell.

This comes by the Prince's Express.

LETTER 31

Luke Reynolds is described in *Prisoners of the '45* as a French lieutenant. He was a captain in Lord John Drummond's Regiment, and presumably came over with Arbuthnot's cargo (see Letters 28 and 29) as an advance party. He was imprisoned in Edinburgh Castle and gaol and was eventually pardoned in October 1748, on condition that he left the country.

The 'Happy Janet' was one of His Majesty King George's sloops, and Lieutenant John Knight, R.N., was in command. He was a constant correspondent of Rear Admiral John Byng, and kept him informed with intelligence reports.

1. Pieces of a Letter I cannot make anything of.

2. Scraps of a Letter to His Royal Highness.

The above are Copys and Pieces of Letters taken from Luke Reynolds, Prisoner, brought on board from 'The Happy Jennett.' He was taken up by the Constables of Kinross, says he was an Officer in the King of France's Service, and came over here in a Vessel from Dunkirk with arms to Montrose 30th Octor. 1745.

Sent me by Lieutent Knight. Novr. 2d. 1745.

Transmitted to the Admiralty 2d of November 1745.

LETTER 32

The following is a letter which seems to show that, although it is frequently reported to the contrary, Prince Charles was quite attractive to the ladies. The 'Lady K.' mentioned may have been the wife of Lord Kilmarnock, who was executed on Tower Hill on 18 August 1746 for his part in the Rising. She was daughter of James, Lord Linlithgow, and later contributed to the defeat of the Government army at Falkirk on 17 January 1746, by diverting General Hawley with her hospitalities at Callendar House, an intrusion forced on her, and much against her inclinations.

Dr Madam: I'm very sensible of the kind concern you express about me and mine in yours I had the favour of last night. I thank God we are all pritty well, better than cou'd have been expected after the many inconveniences attended our coming here but nothing to be complain'd of in these times when there is reason for great fear but still ground of hopes that all will go well trusting in our infinitely Good God who has done great things for us will still bless the first generous and noble undertaking of so compleat a P—— whose merit I cant express. I pray you may reap the benefit of them, and enjoy good health which I'm heartily sorry is so bad at present. But I most hope the best about you and all your concerns, and I assure you, Dr Ma, I'l ever reckon it a happiness to serve you, and whom you mention in particular, that it may soon be in my power to have that opportunity you seem to expect. I am sure I would be most ingrate if I neglected to do wherein capable to serve you and all your greatest concerns which I'l ever do with pleasure. I have not seen Mrs. Sharp but I hear she is much in her ordinary way, but I had the satisfaction to see my favourite Mr. W. G. the other day in health and cheerfully hoping the best. I'm in such confusion and heast that I have much to say. Can add no more but all your friends with me join in our affectionate humble service to you and all with you, dear Madam, adieu. Lady K. desired me to tell you that she granted the Still to Lady Kilconquin [?] thinking you would be done with it or she needed it.

Memo. From Edinbr. to Miss Margaret Sharp in St. Andrews in praise of P . . . . . C . . . . . . Sign'd no body.

LETTER 33

Apparently the delivery of newspapers was rather chaotic during the Prince's occupation of Edinburgh. The garter referred to by the writer may have been one of the Jacobite ones, of which one or two are still in existence, bearing the motto, 'When this you see remember me.'

Dear Will: I received your very obliging epistle of the 24th las night in which you are so good as to give us the News Passing, and a very entertaining description of Mrs. T . . . There is no body in Dundee received a newspaper almost since the P . . . . . came to Edinbr. Pray will either you or Mr. Robertson (who promised me them) cause them be sent regularly. We likewise received yours with the Garter for which the Ladys desire me to return thanks, and assure you that it was applyed accordingly to orders and consequently had the desired effect.

Notwithstanding of the present troubles and confusion there are more people than Mr. T . . . who think of increasing their happiness by dividing their cares. Know then there was another William full as lithe as the former, who married last night a Lady full as lean as the one you mention who (by what I understand) eats a great deal less. These are convenient wives in either war or famine. If the times grow much worse, I shall repent I have not followed their Example, for in spite of publick Calamities, things go on much in the same way at breakfast, Dinner and Supper as when you were here.

All here desire their complements to you and I remain,
Dr Will
Yours sincerely

M . . . . . n Novr. 2d 1745.

Memo. From M . . . . . n to Mr. Willm Douglas, Mercht. in Edinburgh. Novr. 2d 1745. Sign'd by no body.

LETTER 34

The writer of this letter was eighteen-year-old Janet, second daughter of Lord Braco, who had only been married to Sir William Gordon of Park, Aberdeenshire, for five months when she wrote this letter. Her husband had joined the Prince at Perth in September, and had been given his commission as Colonel in Pitsligo's Horse on 18 October at Holyroodhouse. Made one of the Prince's Council in the same month, he was sent over to France with urgent pleas for help, but he was back again in time to be with the Highland army on its march into England, and later at Culloden. He escaped abroad after months of hiding.

After Culloden Lady Gordon was made prisoner, but shortly afterwards she was allowed to go to her mother's house at Braco, where her daughter was born. By the good offices of her parents, who were Whigs, she and her daughter soon joined her husband in France. In March 1749 they were at Boulogne, where their eldest son was born, and in 1750 another son was born at Douai. Sir William was attainted and specially excepted from pardon in the Act of Indemnity in June 1747, and about 1750 he was appointed Lieutenant-Colonel of Lord Ogilvy's Regiment in the French service, which at least kept the family out of poverty, and he was several times given sums of money from the grants made to Prince Charles by the French Government. He died at Douai in June 1751, and Lady Gordon lived in want until 1752, when she returned to Scotland and married George Hay of Mountblairy. Thus he became another 'dearest life.'

The rumour she mentions, that George Keith the Earl Marischal was about to land, was unfortunately untrue. That gentleman had at last decided, having nearly lost his liberty in 1715 and 1719, that he would have done with the plotting of the Stuarts. He took no part in the 1745 Rising, and drifted into peaceful old age with a galaxy of attractive Eastern slaves and the friendship of the Prussian Emperor Frederick.

My Dearest Life: I give you ten thousand thanks for your kind obliging letter, I'l assure my Dearest it was a great cordial to my poor heart who was almost broken before I got your letter. I did not know what to think for I was sure if my Dearest Life had been well he could not been so cruel as to forget me when you are very sensible how distractedly fond I am of you but I'l never be so uneasy again, my Dearest gave me a very good reason for my not hearing. You wrote me of 6000 of the Clans going to join in a two three days. I am afraid my Dear, you'r wrong informed here, for that Base Villain Lovat has not allow'd his men to march as yet. There is a relation of mine kept a Guard upon his Garrison of 140 men, I mean my Uncle. They tell me that Lord Lewis Gordon has been paying him a visit, but what passed between them I don't know. Arachie was sent with a message to my papa, desiring a man of every 100£ rent, the same was to be intimated to Lord Finletor [Findlater] and Aberdeen. I saw a letter from your sister my Lady Forbes. The Master knew nothing of the joining of his North Country friends till the day before he wrote his last letter, but he was a good deal surprized. Lord Morton, his name is Douglas he lives in Kathness [sic] has raised they tell me 140 men for the Elector of Hanover. The Gentleman that brought your last letter to me tells that he saw 17 Sail of Arbroth, and they told him when he came to Montrose that they were assured by a Frigate that came to reconoitre the coast that it was Lord Marshall. But whether it be true or not God alone knows. We can believe nothing, we hear so many lyes, however my Dearest Life we shall keep up a good heart, I hope God will have mercy on us and turn everything out well. I am quite rejoiced in hearing thy Dearest Life is in so good spirits, I hope in God you shall never have reason to be otherways. Its true your numbers is but very small in comparison to the numbers your Enemy has against you, and believe some people they would have it that he has 30,000, but since may tell us that he cant have the half of that number. Some people is so wicked as to say that there will be no landing from France, but its scarce to be believed that the French King should be such a villain after the many assurances he gave the Prince to join him with heart and hand. I shall follow my Dearest Life's example and keep up my spirits, and no more think of that cursed Battle that has so much raked and vexed my mind. I cannot express to my Dearest Life how much I am obliged to you for the promise you made me of taking care of your health, and not venturing yourself in danger but where your Duty necessary calls you. I have a most gratefull sence of your goodness in making me this promise. I assure you it will make me very happy if my Dearest Life keep it, but they alarm me a little by telling me that the Volunteers must be on every desperate attack. If your Duty calls you there what is to become of me? However my Dearest Life I shall obey your Commands and keep up my spirits. How happy would I be if I had only a confirmation of my Lord Marshal's landing. As

63

to your labouring its going very well on all that can be done just now to it. I have caused Mr. Duff write you in what way your Tenants is in, and what he has been doing since you went away. I am to send his letter by Miss Jeany Gordon who goes South Monday or Tuesday. I'm sorry to think my Dearest could think that anything concerning you could be a trouble to me. My Dearest Life may be persuaded that it will add greatly to my happiness if I be capable to serve you in the least. I pray you my Dear write me what will be done with North Lesly. He is asking about £ sterling at this term, as you left no orders about him ere you went away. Neither Mr. Duff nor I would venture to give him anything. He was in one of his mad fits, but I put him of to the term. I beg of you my Dear to write me by first post what you would have done as he will be very soon upon my Barns. As I am to write to you by Carnucies Daughter on Monday, I shall not trouble you with any particulars, but pray my Dearest Life to take care of his dear self, and do nothing that you think may harm your health, a thing that I prize so dear it would be very hard to rob me of by venturing yourself to danger. I wish to God these parties your sent out on may not be dangerous. I could scrible on the whole night to you, I never think but my Dear has as much idle time as myself. I shall have done, only add my sincere good wishes to all my friends. I hope my Dearest Life will ever believe me to be with great truth and Love my Dearest,

Your most obedient and faithfull servant

while I breath.

Park. Novembr. 2d. 1745.

Adieu my Dearest. God bless you and preserve you.
Your aunt Lady Drumwhendle is dead.

My Dearest Life adieu.

Memo. From Park Novr. 2d. 1745 to the Honble Sr. Wm. Gordon of Park. Signed by no body.

The writer of the following letter was quite obviously an enthusiastic Jacobite. He is probably William Cruikshank, from Mearns, the old name for Kincardineshire, and appears in Rosebery's *List*. He is called a 'Sub Tenent'—this may have something to do with the fact that he wishes his service to be given 'to my Landlord and Landlady'—and his act of rebellion was 'Voluntary, carried Arms with the Rebels and was most outrageous.' He was said at the time of the making out of the *List* in May 1746 to be 'lurking,' and what happened to him is not known.

He is a little late with his news about the ships at Montrose and Stonehaven. Between 9 and 19 October four ships from France had landed artillery and stores at these places, and there had been escorted to Edinburgh by the Atholmen and the MacPhersons.

Sir Alexander Bannerman of Elsick, Kincardineshire, 'we hear is coming down from the Camp Lord Lieutenant of this Shire,' is described in Rosebery's *List* as, 'Acted as Lord Lieut of the County of Merns under the Rebels, was active in serving their interest and yet moderate to the Country.' Sir Alexander's mother was a daughter of Sir Alexander MacDonald of Sleat. He was the third baronet, and recruited a regiment for the Prince which was present at Culloden. He escaped to France and died at Paris in 1747.

Dr Comerade: I have given you the trouble of these few lines to let you know that I am in good health at present, wishing that this may find you in the like condition. Your friends are all well, I saw your Mother but two days ago, but we are in the greatest consternation here that can be, and nothing but confusion apeareth upon all hands. We are expecting every day to be taken up for soldiers, for all other places round about us, except this Shire of Mearns, are putting out great numbers of men, and here the greatest part of common people want nothing but are to call them out and head them, but the Gentlemen are all quiet yet except Johnstown and Elsick, the latter we hear is coming down from the Camp Lord Lieutenant of this Shire, and then we expect to be like our neighbours about us, that is appearing in Arms for our King and Country. We hear for certain from the North that

there are whole Parishes that there are not a man left but three
or four that are able to bear arms, so that if this Heroic spirit
continueth among us, you are like to have all Scotland in one
side of the Forth. There [were] four ships here, two at Montrose,
and two at Stonhive [Stonehaven] loaded with Gold and money
in Bars and coine, firelocks, broadswords, and Pistols and five
Brass Cannon and great Quantitys of Ammunition and all manner
of warlike stores. This is a short hint of the news of our country,
be pleased to send me the news of yours and let me know how you
are by the first post. Send me word if you have got my Napkine,
and let me know when you think to be home, and if there are any
Sallys in Renfrie [Renfrew] in this troublesome times, I shall insist
no further but offer my service to you from the hand of yours,
While, Wm. Crookshank.
Balbeyno [Balbegno] Novr. 3d. 1745.

P.S. Give my service our sisters and old Nancy and John Low,
tell him his friends are all well. Give my service to my landlord
and landlady. As for my old Master, I'm not sure but I may have
an opportunity of offering my service to him myself.

Memo. From Wm. Crookshank of Balbeyno to Alexr. McNeil of
Glasgow giving him an acct of four ships land arms and money,
etc.

LETTER 36

This letter refers to the activities of John Gordon of Avochie in
Aberdeenshire and Banffshire. Directly he received on 14 August
1745 the Prince's summons to the raising of the standard five days
later, he immediately set about raising men in the Strathbogie (now
Huntly) district. By November he had managed to bring in some
three hundred, of whom he was given command. In Rosebery's
List he is referred to as a 'Rebell Collonel.' He did not go into England with the Prince, but remained with Lord Lewis Gordon raising
men for the cause. He was at the skirmish of Inverurie in December
1745 when Lord Lewis defeated MacLeod, and at both Falkirk and
Culloden. He escaped to France, and later about 1763, having paid
£500 fine, he returned home to Avochie and died in 1778.

He seems to have annoyed Grant of Achoynany, who is perhaps the Grant mentioned here, as receiving him 'in a manner more sturdy when he would have Levied a Cess,' because elsewhere Grant describes him as 'Lord Lewis Gordon's Prime Minister of Oppression.' The cess was the land tax, but Charles also demanded levy money, 'demanding an able-bodied man sufficiently accoutred in the Highland Dress [plaid, short clothes, hose and shoes] for each £100 Scots of valued rent, or £5 Sterling to raise one. The man was but a pretext, it was the money they wanted. This indeed would have amounted to a very considerable sum; no less than about 5s Ster in the pound off the real rack'd rent [£5 in every £8 6s. 8d.] which exorbitant demand would at any time have been very hard upon Lairds and Tenants, but after two bad crops and so many other losses, was indeed more than they could bear.'

Lord Lewis Gordon was appointed Lord Lieutenant of Aberdeenshire and Banffshire before Charles left Edinburgh in October.

William Duff, Lord Braco, was a large landowner in Aberdeenshire and Banffshire, holding land mostly purchased from the government after the forfeitures in 1715. He was a Whig, and joined Cumberland in 1745.

Dear Sir: Among the various circumstances of affairs at Edinr. of late I'm very anxious to know you and your young folks and how my good friend Mr. Farquharson have far'd, alarm'd you must have been and disconcerted but I hope no more, and as I know the Goodness of your hearts, I conceive that by this time your concern for others frequently engages your mind as I own it does mine. Tis a hardship at this time that the news that are so eagerly sought after are so little to be depended on, what your paper is stuffed with from this country has frequently so little truth in it that it makes one apt to suspect the veracity or partiality of those from other parts. I have little of consequence to write the knowledge of which could amuse you. The papers inform you of some having come to St . . . . y [Strathbogie] and the new L . . . . L . . . . [Lords Lieutenant] raising in this and B . . . . Sh . . . [Banffshire] it was reported in that Country some days ago of the Gr . . ts [Grants] and Fr . . . . s [Frazers] having a design upon them but I hear no more of it. There likewise has been some Report of a foreign force landing but as it shifts from the East to the West Coasts perhaps its indeed no where. Tis said L . . . B . . . o [Lord Braco] did not at all relish a demand that was made a few days ago by A . . . . y [Avochy] and that A . . . . y was received by Gr . . t [Grant] in a manner more sturdy when he would have lev . . d [levied] a C . . ss [Cess]. We hear likewise of a great forwardness of the A . . y [Army] from London and in the present conjecture I believe no man of sense in Edinr. or London would find fault with an honest Scot or Britains saying to what end will God almighty bring all these commotions! My only happiness is that I rely on the wisdom and Goodness of the directing hand and humbly wish well to my Country, but when or how, Religion and Policy forbid me to conjecture. If I have a wish for particulars it is that Heaven would regard the honesty of every heart in mercy. You'l say I'm very serious. I have I assure you been more so of late than I thought of being this side my grand Climaterick. I have of late heard of no stop to letters, if this of mine be open'd by any one, if it contains nought but a few sentiments of an honest tho anxious Briten, let him suffer it to pass to the honest country man to whom it is directed for if he be a good man you and I are his friend. I'l be glad to hear from you soon and write what you think proper. Be not too sparing except in reflections which may be ill tim'd. Please also acquaint the Post Office that the Courant has not been sent me these two months and cause that or some other paper be sent forthwith, send me anythings printed with you. My wife and sister offer you the complements of Friends and your young friend is a fine fellow, I assure you another will arrive very soon its to be hoped. My heart as well as the usuall stile bids me subscribe myself, Dr Sir,

Your affect. Friend and faithfull humble servt whom you cant fail to find out.

At my own house
Novr. 4th 1745.
Fail not to write first post.

Memo. Letter without a name from Aberdeen to Mr. James Hay, writer to the Signet at his house in the Fleshmarket Close, Edinr.

This letter may have been written by James Anderson of Boyndie, one of whose letters appears in A. and H. Tayler's *Jacobites of Aberdeenshire and Banffshire in the Forty-Five*. He was of the Whiggish persuasion.

Dr Sir: I had occasion to be at Miln of Tillinaught [Banffshire] upon Saturday where I spent several hours with your mother and Sister who are in good health and vastly easier since they heard from you. They gave me the enclos'd which I promised to forward to you. I cannot promise it will certainly reach you, but if this does I doubt not it will also, and which is all I can do to implement my promise, I shall take care they be put into the Bagg. We are continually harras'd here with plying partys carrying off our horses and extorting Cess and Excise so that our Country at present is very far from being desirable. Your mother told me that as your Business is presently at a stand, you had some thought of coming North and I believe you would stay with her constantly or for most part. You could live cheaper here but then I'm vastly aprehensive you might run some risque, by the way, as it is at present infested with people of different opinions, and as you might possibly be unknown to all of them, be suspected by all and of consequence be ill used by them.

If you could safely correspond with me and write me your news it would be very obliging, or if you cant do this at present to do it as soon as your strangers are gone and you are under no Restraints further. More especially I would beg that if an Action happen soon you would acquaint me by first post to what side the Victory inclines, only if it inclines to the wrong side I shall forgive you to be silent for ill tidings come soon enough when they come. But if it shall please God whose is the Event of Battle to declare for that party I wish well to, it will signally oblige me to signify the same to me by first post.

I am very sincerely Dr Sir,

Yours etc. J.A.

B . . . . ie [Boyndie]. Novr. 4th 1745.

Memo. From J. A. of B . . . . ie to Mr. Thos Ruddock writer in Edinr.

LETTER 38

A very interesting letter showing the difficulties of travel in Scotland at the time of the '45. The minister seems to have been a man with a dry sense of humour.

Aberdeen 4th Novr. 1745.

Dr Friend: There is so little entertaining in a journey from E to A that you may spare yourself the trouble of reading till you come to the two three last lines of this letter, the sum total being that I arrived here on Saturday night safely. Wednesday forenoon mounted stop'd on Cramon [Cramond] Bridge. Questions from whence, who are you? Where going from Edinr? You may see my Caracter in my Dress, I am going about the Dutys of my Office—He is certainly a Minister—Sir, you may pass when you please. But whence are you two other Gentlemen etc? I found my Band was of use not only to myself but to my two companions who were dismissed readily. At twelve was happily conducted on board the Happy Jannett and happily dismissed with a volley from all her guns. I had more joy in thinking these were innocent blasts and could not hurt our boat than if they had been discharged in honour of the Pretr.

Din'd plentifully at North Ferry on Cakes and Ale because there was nothing else to be got, no not Butter and Eggs, nor Cheese. Mounted again with a Runner at my foot. By moon light fell in on the Road to Leslie with a young woman who was properly dressed and walked as stately thro' the Gutters as ever Diana did thro' the woods—Conversation—Have the Highland men been here? I fancy you ask that as being a favourer of theirs —It may be so, but pray who is Minister of this place (King Glassy)—May a one ask what they know full well—Really I know not his name—It is Mr. Currie honest man of whom every body has heard, he is a sweet preacher, I hear him every week— Have you no Minister at Leslie where Lord Rothes has his place?— O yes we have, and the one is a Seceder, but you know one likes to go where they are most edifyed (—Apart to my Boy) who is this Gentleman?—I know not but believe he is a Minister by his Coat.

By this time we were got to the Village and at parting realy I have been very luckie (said she) in good Company this time of night on the Road, I wish you good journey, Farewell.

My landlady received me kindly put on a fire made ready supper.

I drank a snaker with my Landlord who by the description the Boy had given him of the young woman told me that she was the only Wh—— in the Town. Slept sound—mounted, came without any remarkable to Arbroth [*sic*] Thursday night. Friday dismal rain and wind, keep'd the Coast road all the way to Bervie, wet to the skin, but found small pleasure in observing the vast huge Rocks, and seeing the foaming surges lash the sounding shore. Slept well at Bervie and next day got to Aberdeen. Not half an hour in Town when everybody heard of it in spite of my endeavours to conceal it. Messages, Company, etc. Sunday preach'd and six finitur tabula.

I find I will get a feather Bed to purchase here and Blankets too. Shall write more at leisure to Mrs. Stuart. Must have good Chimney Tongs etc for a Dining Room, a small mirror for adjusting my wig and Band if to be had easily. Remember my Scrivitore and see that the Brushes and Locks be good. Any utensils for a kitchen, I desire Mrs. Stuart may have her eye on. I have writ you the above believing by this time your fears of poor Gibbie are quit over. Pray let me know how he is and learn first to submitt and then to trust in Providence. All your news let me have. I hope the Coast is or will soon be clear. Send my Complements to Mr. Dunbar and tell him I am well. I forgott to speak of Bed And Table Linnen tho as necessary as anything.

I am etc. R.P.

Item. Pair good candlesticks (brass) and snuffers. I have some new shirts making at Dalkeith which will be sent to you, pray forward them with my books.

Memo. Mr. R. P. at Aberdeen to Mr. George Stuart, Professor of Humanity in Edinr.

Lord George Murray had of course joined the Prince: MacLeod of MacLeod and Sir Alexander MacDonald of Sleat (see Letter 30) were for the Government. Of MacLeod, Murray of Broughton wrote: 'Never did man betray so basely as MacLeod,' after stating that he had given a written promise to aid the Prince whenever he landed. This statement of Murray's is borne out by family tradition. Andrew Lang wrote in *The Companions of Pickle*, quoting from MacKenzie's *History of the MacLeods*:

'Miss MacLeod of MacLeod, Dunvegan Castle, remembers having seen in the family charter-chest an interesting correspondence between His Royal Highness and MacLeod, in which Norman "invited the Prince to come over several months before he arrived" but the letters have since disappeared, and the family knows nothing as to where they have gone to.'

Lovat at least sent his son with a proportion of the Frazers, who joined the Prince in December. MacLeod neither came himself, nor did he send his son.

Portsoy 4th Novr. 1745.

Dr Sir: I sent your letter to your friend Robt. Innes with your draught on him, but he refused the same as he says he has ordered you paymt at Edinr. You can take your own method in reimbursing me an other way. I beg in return to hear some of your news. I'm quite anxious on accot of our country men so deeply engaged. Except what we have in the publick news we have nothing here, and you know they are not much to be depended on on either side. We hear of L. Murray and other persons of distinction joining the P . . . ce and that McD . . . . d [McDonald] and McLeod are actually with you and the Frazers, pray is it so, or what is new since I came off? What is the Generall opinion of the Cause now? You need not sign your answer so that it cannot affect you and I beg for God's sake you'l be plain. We live here like Hermits, I have neither heard the voice or seen the face of a stranger since I came home. Your mother and sister are well, I saw the last at Hallowfair and told her I left you well. I am, Dr Sir,

Your affect. humble Servt.
James Robertson.

Memo. From Mr. Robertson to Mr. Ruddock writer in Edinr.

LETTER 40

James Farquharson of Balmoral had been 'out' in 1715, when he had held the rank of major, and was A.D.C. to the Earl of Mar. Married to Marjory Leith, he brought the Farquharsons in 1745 to join the Prince. He was seen to 'march towards Dundee with about 500 men to gather up the excise and Land Stent for the rebel Prince.' Wounded at Falkirk, he went home, but was arrested long after Culloden, being excepted from pardon in the Act of Indemnity, and in November 1748 he submitted a memorial stating that he had been forced to join the Prince in October 1745, and had left his service in February 1746. He was convicted, but released, and he died in 1753.

Francis Farquharson of Monaltrie, commonly called 'Baron Ban' because of his long fair hair, joined the Prince after Prestonpans with some thirty men. He did not go to England, but was present at Inverurie, Falkirk, and Culloden, where he was captured. He was tried, pleaded guilty, and was sentenced to death in London, but was reprieved the day before his execution, probably mainly owing to the petition of Alexander Robertson, Baron Reid, a very ardent Whig. He was soon afterwards pardoned on condition that he went abroad, but this was altered to one binding himself to confine himself to one place in England as directed by the King. He was therefore kept a partial prisoner at Berkhampstead until 1766, when he was released. In 1775 he was allowed to rent some of his forfeited estates, and he died a model landlord, at Monaltrie in 1790.

Charles Gordon of Blelack was present at Inverurie, Falkirk, and Culloden. He is stated in Rosebery's *List* to have been a captain and to have 'forced men out on the Earl of Aboyne's estate.' Wounded at Culloden, he 'skulked' in Aberdeenshire, and was never taken. He eventually quietly returned to his burnt home and died there in 1785.

Patrick Duguid of Auchinhove took part in the 1715 Rising when only fifteen years old. No measures were taken against him and, succeeding to Auchinhove in 1731, he declared for Prince Charles in 1745, and in the November of that year brought thirty or forty men to Aberdeen. He was wounded at Inverurie in December, and was present at Culloden in April 1746. Escaping after the battle, he could not return home to Auchinhove as it was occupied by Government troops under Captain Hardy (see Letter 64), so he hid in the neighbourhood, his wife Amelia living at Auchinhove with three small children. Hardy eventually ordered the burning of the house without any warning. Although he never received any redress for this wanton act, Duguid seems never to have left Scotland, and to have been pardoned in 1755. He died in April 1777.

Of a Jacobite family, James Moir of Stoneywood joined the Prince just before he reached Edinburgh, and from him obtained a commission to raise men. He at once returned to Aberdeenshire and raised a battalion of infantry known as 'Stoneywood's Regiment,' of which Lord Lewis Gordon was honorary Colonel. With his regiment he was with the Highland army on their march into England, and is said to have been one of the few who counselled marching on to London at the Council at Derby. After Culloden he remained hidden in the neighbourhood of Stoneywood for some time, and then, under the assumed name of James Jamieson, he took up the trade of cobbling in a remote part of Buchan at the house of one John Clark. In November 1746 with John Gordon of Glenbucket and others he sailed for Norway. Subsequently joined by his wife he was sixteen years in exile, eventually returning to Scotland and dying in 1784.

George Mackenzie, Earl of Cromarty, joined the Prince at Perth, was employed in collecting money in Fife, and was present at the Battle of Falkirk. He was put in command of operations against Lord Loudoun, but was not successful. The day before Culloden he was taken by the Sutherland Militia, and committed to the Tower. In July 1746 he was tried and sentenced to death with forfeiture, but he was reprieved in August. In 1748 he was allowed to leave the Tower and live at the house of a messenger, and in October 1749 he was pardoned on condition of his confining himself to such part of England as his Majesty should direct. He died in London in September 1766 in a greatly impoverished state.

Dr George: Mr. Farquharson of Balmurral has raised already 200 men for the P . . . . . and Monaltrie, Blelack and Auchnahove are raising men fast and are getting a number. Lord Lewis Gordon who is Lord lieutent of Aberdeen and Banff Shires in his Brothers land is getting one Man of each Pleugh by which he will have a number of men. Stonnywood one of his Deputys has write to all the Gentlemen within 12 Miles of Aberdeen to have a man ready for every hundred pound of valued Rent, well cloth'd having a plaid, but I do not hear of any thats observing that Direction. It's thought there must be some kind of Force used before that order be obeyed since none will voluntarily raise men that go not out themselves.

I was inform'd for certain that Earle Cromarty was on the head of his McKenzies and that the greater part of the McIntosh's are on their way to the P . . . . . and that the Frazers were all rendezvous'd and were to go, and that was thought Sir Alexr. McDonald with his men would go but it was doubted if McLeod would go.

4th Novembr. 1745.

Memo. To Mr. George Innes at the Stamp Office Edinburgh. Signed no body.

LETTER 41

A letter from a lady who is obviously worried about clothes. Bellfield was probably the Bairds' residence at Springbank in Lanarkshire.

November the 5th.

Dr B: Yours of the 1st instant came to me this night, another Epistle you mention has not. I rejoyce you had a safe journey and that the end of it was so satisfactory. I was told today that you are at Bellfield and not at P . . . . or N. M. as you once intendd. The day after you left, B. J. sent a servant thither with a letter to you and what you write for, if thats not come to your hands you'l find it on your return hither which I long for with impatience. All here are well. I'm quite recovered my late illness. I will add no more but that I am with the sincerest affects.

yours

As you are so volatile I dont know where to direct, If this reaches you its well. Be sure to acquaint me when I shall send the Chaire for you to B and be so good as to inquire for my white gown, and get for G black shoes or in short whatever you can. O. B. gives you the best wishes, mine I offer to all my friends, adieu.

The Carrier is gone over this week with him, I expect my grey Sack.

Memo. To Mrs. Paterson to be left at Lady Baird's house in Canongate Edinr. not signed.

LETTERS 42 AND 43

The James Brand mentioned in the following letter as having deserted his wife and children to join the Prince is said in Rosebery's *List* to have been the son of Alexander Brand, watchmaker of Canongate Edinburgh, and to have 'commanded a party of Rebel Hussars and assisted in levying the Cess at Selkirk etc.' In *The Prisoners of the '45*, he is described as a major in Baggot's Hussars. He was taken the day after Culloden, and at his trial in September he asked to be transported in lieu of the death penalty. His plea was refused and he was hanged at Carlisle on 18 October 1746.

Mr. Watson.

Sir: I shall be glad to hear of your Spouse getting well to Edinr. and how all goes with you at this present troublesome time, for here we are in fears night and day. James Brand watchmaker who I recommend to your care, took on with Lord Ogilvie that night in Montrose and went straight along with him without seeing me, his wife or any body, or ever writing since to any. We hear he is now one of the P . . . cs Life Guard, and I have got the wife and two Boys to take care of, so I entreat you'l do for them what you can in getting up her Rents or any other debts are due her

as she will inform you by the enclosed. Pray give my service to Doctor John Cainkide [?] and let him know that nothing else would have hindered my sending his haddocks but this hurry that no man is bale from his house an hour. Please call for James Brand and as we are assured he lives in plenty if he has not a mind to send something to his wife and ffamily leaving them so destitute. This with my service to your Spouse and my wife and all friends, expecting your answer pr first and if anything further be wanting let us know, I remain with respect, Dr Sir, Your most humble, James Arbuthnott.
Caberline [Cambuslang?] 5th November 1745.

Sir: I sent a letter to you by my husband, but he going off in such hurry without biding farewell to me or any else, I do not know whether it came to your hand or not. Its giving you power to lift some money belonging to me by my Father as being equal with the rest in his Testament. It was six years after his death ere we agreed on the selling of it, of wch I want my part of six years rent, two guineas due to me by Billy Twaddle, forty six pounds Scots money by Henry Young, six pound stirling money by my Brother in law Mr. Mubrey. All this people live at Mid Calder. Mubrey and Young live in my fathers house. The Testament is either in my Brothers hand who lives at Leith or my sister Mrs. Mercis who lives at —— besides Leak. My brothers is Jame Jameson a Sailor, this you'l oblige Sir
Helen Tomson.

Memo. From James Arbuthnott and Helen Tomson to Mr. John Watson Writer in Edinr. the first acquainting him that James Brand went with Lord Ogilvie and is now a Life Guard man to the P . . . ce.

LETTERS 44–46

Three short notes from men in the Highland army to their wives.

In Rosebery's *List* Thomas Forbes, the writer of Letter 44, is described as a 'Vintiner' of Peterhead who 'joined the Rebel Army at Edinburgh.' Nothing further is known about him.

The writer of Letter 45 is presumably William Scott of Roy Stuart's Regiment who, it is stated in *The Prisoners of the '45*, was taken at the capture of Carlisle on 30 December 1745. He was tried at York in October 1746, found guilty, and sentenced to death, but reprieved. He was pardoned in July 1748 on condition of enlistment.

Alexander Forbes, the writer of Letter 46, is described as a 'Stabler' of Peterhead in Rosebery's *List*, who 'went to the Rebellion a servant to Wm. Scott late of Auchtydonald on 1st Octr. 1745' (presumably the writer of Letter 45). It may be that this is the Alexander Forbes mentioned in *The Prisoners of the '45*, who acted as servant to John Hamilton, Governor of Carlisle, and who was taken at the surrender of that place. To his shame he turned King's Evidence against many of the Carlisle prisoners, and was released.

'Capt. More' may refer to Charles Moir, younger brother of James Moir of Stoneywood, who was a captain in Lord Lewis Gordon's Regiment. There were two Volums 'out' in the '45, James and Thomas, sons of William Volum of Peterhead, and as both are described as 'surgeons' in Rosebery's *List*, they were probably medical students. James after being abroad for some time returned to Peterhead, but Thomas was probably killed, as he is not heard of after the Rising.

The Highland army divided into two columns at Dalkeith on 1 November, and the Prince's column, with Lord George Murray as second-in-command, halted at Kelso on 5 November.

Kelso 5th Novemr. 1745.
My Dearest: Ye have a receipt of Jas Jollyes and likewise a receipt to make the fashionable liquor Huskie. We are now a fine Army composed with the best and daringest men from all places (except from Peterhead only two) and every moment joiners. I have no fears but by God's blessing we'l have a merry meeting.

I am my Dearest
Your most affect. husband, Thos. Forbes.
Auchdonald, Capt. More.
Mr. Volum and Alexr. Forbes are well.

My Dearest: Your brother George is to join the Army Thursday and how soon he arrives shall write you. I am, my Dearest,
Your affect. husband
William Scott.

My Dearest: I have been on a partie at Hamilton and Glasgow and the Army was march'd or we came up. Sandy has been a litle sick but is recovered. I had the favour of Mr. Forbes Letter, being in heast.
Alexr. Forbes.

Memo. Letters from Thos. Forbes, Willm Scott and Alexr. Forbes from Kelso to Mrs. Forbes at Peterhead 5 Novr. 1745. All these three letters are written on one sheet of paper.

LETTERS 47 AND 48

The writer of these letters was William Gibbon, described in Rosebery's *List* as a merchant of Stonehaven, of Pitsligo's Horse, 'servant to Wm. Menzies of Pitfodder [Pitfodels], a rebel.' Taken after Culloden, he was still in Tilbury Fort in May 1747, and his ultimate fate is unknown. Actually William Menzies of Pitfodels, although 'out' in 1715, took no active part in the 1745 Rising, except to compel those whom he could to take up arms in the Prince's cause. His eldest son, Gilbert, was 'out' in '45, as were his five other sons, and he was present with the Highland army throughout the campaign, eventually escaping to France. He was excepted from pardon in 1748, and, as he had formerly served in France, he received a pension from the French government in November 1748.

Kelso 5th Nov. 1745.
Dr. Wife: When I wrote you last from Edinr. I forgot to give you orders to clear with the Tenants upon their house rents, which by this I order you to do until I return, and your receipt to them shall be as good as if it were from me. Wm. Reid is due me at this Martinmas three pound, John Martin £3.10., Peter Cushnie at Whitsunday last £26.13.4. and at this Martinmas

79

£10 for his house and £1.6. is for his yard. John Cergill at this Martinmas a years rent £22 and 20 shillings ballance of his former rent. He has a discharge of the rent but as he wanted this twenty shill to pay me up I trusted to his word, I do not think he'l swear to the contrary. The two little houses att this Martinmas at £2.10 earn all which money call for and pay the Lady Bridfeard with. I am due Peter Cushnie a shop acct. all owe that in the first end of his Meal. Thos. Stead rents me a Boll malt at Ly and Mr. Ogilvie is due me acct. for malt. I do not mind me upon my tongue, he has an acct. himself, you'l charge him £7. for each Boll. Ye must manadge all things as frugal as possible and see to pay all my Debts with my effects untill such time as it shall please God in his good Providence to return me home which I pray God may be soon.

I am Dear Wife your Loving husband while
Willm. Gibbon.

P.S. I have left here with Mr. McLellan the Episcopil Minister here my pistoles (having got a new pair). Every body here is speaking very badly of Mr. Leslie's behaviour at this time. We must read some people not as they speak but as they behave and act.

Send this part of the   Kelso 5th November 1745.
Letter to F. Urq.
Sir: I wrote you from Edinr. the 31st last to which I refer you. Saturday at 8 at night 24 horse of Pitsligo's men of which I was one marched from Dalkeith and arrived here Sunday night. Yesterday the P . . . ce with about 4000 Highlanders arrived here. He march'd all day at the head of them in his Boots. No man in the Army undergoes so much fatigue and nane upholds better. He is imitating Chas. the 12th of Sweden and for what is yet seen about him he'l be the greatest man of the two. This day we rest here and tomorrow we march for England to fight General Wade who we hear is eleven thousand including four thousand militia and we little above seven thousand if we be that as I do not think we are. Our heavy Bagage and fine train of Artiliry with

the rest of the Arms is past the Twide at a foord about 16 miles above this, and to morrow we are to join and then march in quest of General Wade who is at Newcastle. Saturday last there was a Proclamation read at the Market place here, signed G. Wade by His Maj's. order offering pardon to all of us that would lay down his arms and return home. None of us has accepted his kind offer. If he were not sore afraid he would not make such an offer, especially to those that does not thank him for it. Before the end of next week we expect to be up with Wade and decide Englands fate, when if I survive, I shall write a full account of the Action untill such time I must remain Sir,

Your most humble servt.

Wm. Gibbon.

Memo. Letter from Wm. Gibbon Mercht. in Stonhive [Stonehaven] to his wife write from Kelso, as also anoyr. Letter to be delivered by Mrs. Gibbon to F. Ur.

LETTER 49

A cautious merchant's letter.

6 November, 1745.

Our best yarn has of late fal'n to 21 and 20d pr. spindle, since I have ventured to buy up some 100 sps. in expectation of it's being better in sometime, as it certainly would were we to have peaceable times. But as it's possible the contrary might cause it yet be lower in price, beg you'l do me the favour to consult my good friends anent it and write me their opinion as soon as possible you can, particularly B. Mend, B. Allen, Will. Sterling, G. Brown, I hope will both with his acquaintances anent it. Please desire him to acquaint Mr. Graham that none of the stockings is as yet disposed of, that they are not sought now untill the Spring. Mr. Graham recommended me to a Gentleman who used to deal considerably with J. Smith in Gam [?] whom I promised to advise the prices about this time, but I've forgot his name. Mr. Graham will remember it. Coud wish Mr. Donaldson and Hugh Niven were likeways advised the fall of our Yarn. I've done the [?] work a considerable sum against Janr. first as he's not great occasion for money at present. Desire you'l pay in to Mr. Flint what money was designed to send me and see it's mark'd on the back of my Bill. The Pack of Leather is not yet come to hand, and would gladly know whether Leather is not altered in price since summer. This is a good deal of trouble I put you to but shall not make any Apology at present. As for news since I last wrote you, there is only two more items since that time. Our Lord Lieutnts. by their Deputs are busy all over this country raising the Militia of every Parish, like a man for every Plough or thereby. Our Burroughs are not yet raised. Vast northness continues non liquid. Its reported here that last week the P . . . . . left Edinr. to disperse a gathering of Dutch etc thats said to be forming against him about Newcastle. Others will have it that a considerable Army from England are come down that Length, but this meets with little credit. No alteration here since I last wrote, all at present in good health (Blessed be God) and I am very sincerely yours—you know my hand.

P.S. Please notice that I dont think it needfull to let any body know that I've any considerable parcel of yarns by me, but only that it just now sells at the prices as above.

Memo. Letter to Mr. Patrick Letham, Inkeeper in Bridge Gate, Glasgow. Signed no body.

LETTER 50

George Gordon of Hallhead, to whom the following letter is addressed by his sister, is described in Rosebery's *List* as having 'carried Arms the whole Rebellion, and was Secretary to Lord Pitsligo.' In February 1746 his house in Aberdeen, where his wife, Amy Bowdler, and child, Bob, aged twelve (mentioned in the postscript to the letter), were living, was occupied by General Hawley, who, with his usual disregard of either persons or property, stole most of her movable goods, having the audacity to pack up 'every bit of china I had, which I am sure would not be bought for two hundred pounds, all my beding [*sic*] and table linen, every book, my repeating-clock (which stood by the bed in which he lay every night), my worked screen every ragg of Mr. Gordon's clothes, the very hat, breeches, nightgown, shoes and what shift there was of the child's, 12 teaspoons, strainer and tongs, the japened board on which the chocolate and coffee cups stood, and put them on board a ship in the night time directed to himself at Holyrood House at Edinburgh. The flutes, music and my cane he made presents of . . . even my empty bottles he took.'

George Gordon escaped after Culloden and got to France. In 1747 he was excepted from pardon in the Act of Indemnity, and in 1748 a true bill of High Treason was found against him. He died in France.

'Mr. R. Sandilands' was probably the Robert Sandilands, writer, who is described in Rosebery's *List* as having been 'Captain in the Rebel Service was in England, Falkirk and Culloden, now in the Highlands.' He joined Charles in Edinburgh in October 1745, and had a company in the Duke of Perth's Regiment. After Culloden he got to Sweden. He was a member of the Craibstone family, possibly a son of Lady Craibstone's, judging by the instructions in this letter with regard to forwarding correspondence.

Aberdeen the 6th of Novemr.

My Dr. Brother: Not knowing how to direct for you I have beg'd the favour of Lady Crabston to forward this under her cover to her son, who I hope will find you out. God grant it may meet you in that state of mind and body I wish. It has you may believe afforded me no small satisfaction to hear tho' but a second hand of you, and that you have been so well, but God only knows the many anxious days and hours I have past since I parted with you. But it matters little what I be or how I be so long as God Allmighty of his infinite Goodness and Mercy preserves and protects you and your just and Righteous Cause. May he of his infinit Goodness Crown and prosper you and all of you with compleat success here and for ever more is my constant and most sincere petition you may believe. It would be a great act of Charity to let me hear a line from you Dr. Br., if you can grant my petition do it. We are sometimes here lifted up with good news but alas as often depres'd. God help us and direct and guid you in every step. As I'm quit uncertain if this will find you shall add no more but that I ever am most sincerely your affectionate sister,

J. Gordon.

P.S. My sister and Bob and all your friends here are very well. Pray give my Complements to all friends with you. If your so good as to bestow a line on me give it to Mr. R. Sandilands.

Memo. From J. Gordon of Aberdeen to her Brother George Gordon, Esqr. of Hallhead.

LETTER 51

William Ogilvy, concerning whose affairs the following letter was written, appears in Rosebery's *List* as 'Brother to Auchires— joined the Pretender's son at Edinburgh,' and was the son of James Ogilvy of Auchtires, and younger brother of Alexander Ogilvy who went with Lord Pitsligo, his guardian, and others to join Charles at Edinburgh. Nothing is known of William's adventures in the '45, but afterwards he went to America, and settled in Virginia, where he died in 1750.

Aberdeen 6th Novemr. 1745.

Mr. David Fish,

Sir: I suppose the present commotions is the occasion you have never yet forwarded our last order, should you get any occasion by sea I wish they were sent. This serves chiefly to advise that I understand there is in your Custody a Box directed for Wm. Ogilvie of this place. As he is now given over dealing in our way I have an order from Mr. Handyside of London to receive for his Account that Box which was sent by him to Mr. Ogilvie. It contains 7 pieces of plain silks and fourteen silk Plads. I have enclosed a letter to Mr. Ogilvie, but as he is now in the Prince's Army I'm afraid you'l be at a loss to know how it should be forwarded. However it avails but litle, should you have the Box, and no arrestment yet laid in your hands. I have got this consent

84

of Mr. Ogilvie's Trustees that the Box I should receive on giving
you an Obligation to free you from any trouble whatsoever. I
therefore hope on receipt of this you write me and in the interim
give these Goods in to Mr. Chas. Chyne Merchnt. in Edinr.
which will be doing a singular obligation to us and piece of
Justice to Mr. Handyside of London.

I am,

your most humble servt. James Burnett.

Memo. From James Burnett of Aberdeen to David Fish of Leith.

LETTER 52

This letter is from Amy Gordon (*née* Bowdler) to her husband,
George Gordon of Hallhead (see Letter 50). It is beautifully written
in script. She it was who had the trouble with Hawley when he was
quartered at her house in February 1746.

The 'Mr. Ross of Gellan' mentioned may be James Ross, senior,
of Stoneywood's Regiment, who, according to Rosebery's *List*, was
a 'Sheriff Officer. Carried arms the whole Rebellion and is now
Prisoner at Inverness.' He was sent to London and turned King's
Evidence against Francis Farquharson and others (see Letter 40).

The 'Mr. Moir of Longmay' was William Moir of Lonmay, and
uncle of James Moir of Stoneywood (see Letter 40). He joined
Charles in Edinburgh and was appointed deputy-governor of Aberdeen under Lord Lewis Gordon. He is described in Rosebery's *List*
as 'Factor to the Countess of Errol. Joined the Pretender's son at
Edinr. was appointed Governor of Aberdeen where he Collected
or caused to be Collected the Revenues of Excise and Customs and
the Land Tax and did everything in his Power for the Interest of
the Pretender in the most active manner.' He was excepted from
pardon in the Act of Indemnity, 1747, and in the following year a
true bill of High Treason was found against him in his absence. He
died, probably on the Continent, in 1752.

On Monday the fourth of this instant I received a Letter from my
Dearest Dear George which was dated Delkeith the 28th of October.

That I was heartily glad to see it you may easily judge because in your absence I have no pleasure but the thoughts of seeing you again and in the meantime hearing from you which I had not done since Mr. Leith came here till last Sunday when Mr. Ross of Gellan came to see me and told me he saw you very well. Stoneywood nor any of the Gentlemen that have come from Edinr. have wasted any time in coming to see me, tho' I sent Mr. Petrie word that I should be glad if he would come, and I sent to Mr. Fullerton to ask him how he did. He sent me word that you were well but that he was so ill he could not come to see me, for he was just going into the Country to try to recover his health. I am prodigiously surprised that you do not receive any Letters from me, for once every week have I wrote ever since you went away. They have all been franked by Sr. Arthur and directed to Mr. George Sandilands Merchant, to the care of Mr. Andrew Burnett writer to the Signett, and fancy that if they are enquired for they will be to be had. However as I had at your request a very civil Epistle from Mr. P. Gordon dated the first of this month have enclosed this to him, which hope he will be able to get conveyed to you. For if he cant do it I will not write again it being to no purpose to spend my Eyes and time in flattering myself that I am giving my George pleasure, when alas he do's not receive them which indeed I think a great hardship nor can my imagination find out what becomes of them. But as I am sure that you have not failed writing as often as I mention dare say you do not doubt the truth of it whatever way they are disposed of. In your last you refer me to the bearer of it for news. As the bearer was the Post, I sent everywhere to borrow the Newspaper to see what I could find there, and by that see that you are still in an increasing way which Almighty God grant you may continue to be wherever you go. Its said here that your party is going Southward. Oh how my hopes and fears increase yet when I reflect on the Justice of the undertaking. Check myself for not looking forward on the many advantages that has already happened for which we ought to be thankfull and endeavour to do our utmost that we may not be look'd on as quite unworthy of futur Blessings and Success. Mr. Moir of Longmay [Lonmay] has just been to see me. He was in heast but stayed long enough to raise my Spirits by assuring me that you was very well and that everything went just as it was to be wished for. His hand is tyed up with the wound he got at Perth. How fortunate it was that those Gentlemen happen'd to come there that day, for tho' the Loss might not have been so considerable as it would have been represented, yet some disappointment it would certainly have been. I have had two letters from my brother who says he longs much to see Mr. Mercer and you, but cant write any news from the place where he is and they get none from Scotland, so we must content to have short letters till we meet, which God grant may soon be is the hearty wish and prayer of your Princess. Bob is very well, and sends his Duty. Mr. Gerhard and the Doctor and Mr. Gray are very much yours. Mr. Moir tells me he thinks you will not be gone so soon as some People talk of, but whenever you go remember to write to me as often as you can, for if I cant have the opportunity of doing the same to you, yet your Letters will be a means of keeping me well tho I can not tell you that I am so. I was yesterday to see Mrs. Mercer which is the only time I have been out since you went.

A. G.

Aberdeen November 6th 1745

Memo. From A. G. (Amy Gordon) to George Gordon Esqr. of Hallhead.

LETTER 53

This letter is written to John Hamilton of Sandstown, near Huntly, of whom Rosebery's *List* has this: 'Governour of Carlisle for the Rebels and there made prisoner.' Factor to the Duke of Gordon and over sixty years of age, he joined Charles early, raised a body of one hundred mounted men, and marched them to Inverurie, where he forced the magistrates to attend the reading of the Prince's manifesto. At Aberdeen, when the Provost refused to drink the Prince's health, he forced a glass of wine down his throat. On the capture of Carlisle he was made Governor, and when Carlisle was finally left to its fate, he was made Governor of the Castle, and Francis Townley Governor of the Town. He negotiated the surrender of the town to Cumberland on 30 December 1745, and was then taken to London and lodged in Newgate. He was tried, found guilty, and executed on Kennington Common on 28 November 1746, his servant Alexander Forbes giving evidence against him (see Letter 46). His head was one of those which were sent up to adorn the gates of Carlisle.

'Your old Master' was the third Duke of Gordon, who came out on the Government side in November 1745. His brother was Lord Lewis Gordon, one of the Prince's most active supporters. The Duke of Gordon was said to be very much waiting to see 'which way the cat jumped,' a tradition which seems to be supported by the fact that he gave 'my Lord Pitsligo the bay horse which he rides.'

Dr. John: I received yours but can make nothing of it for you, for there is no Gentleman staying in this Country but what is ready and young. I heard that your old Master did want to know where ye was, which I have let him know, but has not goten any word as yet, but I hear he is coming to this Town very soon. They have taken two horse from him and he gave my Lord Pitsligo the Bay horse which he rides. They took the grey horse. He has been but three Times in Town since ye went away, and for this place you never seed such an Uproar as what is here just now, and I doubt it will be worse. Hallhead is at the Camp and two servants with him. I have no more to say just now but wishes you well, and give if it be in my power to do you a favour ye may be sure of it, but till there be a settlement I can say nothing but I am your assured friend

Will: Johnston.

Aberdeen Novr. 6th 1745.

P.S. All friends and well wishers here is well.

Memo. From Willm. Johnston at Aberdeen to John Hamilton at Edinburgh.

LETTER 54

This letter was written on 6 November. The Prince and his army crossed the Esk into England on 8 November.

Edinr. November the 6th 1745.

Dr. Cousin: I wrote you on Monday 1st requesting the favour of your Servant as mine has thought fit to desert me. And this comes to tell you that the Kinghorn Ferry is now open and that he may come that way, the sooner he set out the better. Pray acquaint me if your Father got a short letter I wrote him the Monday after the Battle Prestonpans, 21 [September]. My Complements with all here to the Honest Lady, to him, and to my Cousins, I am very sincerely, Dr. Cous, your most obedient servt.

Da. Anderson.

P.S. No news yet since the Army march'd South. God send him good for much is at stake.

Memo. From Da: Anderson at Edinr. to Mrs. Blair at Inchyrae to be forwarded by Mr. Miller, Town Clerk from Perth.

LETTER 55

Another enthusiastic letter about the Prince in Edinburgh. The Duke of Perth's house, one of those which the writer says was plundered, was in the Canongate.

General Guest was in 'general military command' of the castle for the Government and he was eighty-five years old at this time. Lord Mark Kerr was the Honorary Governor of the castle, while General Preston, a youngster of eighty-six, was Deputy-Governor and Commandant. After Prestonpans, Guest became Commander-in-Chief in Scotland until superseded by Hawley at the end of December.

My Dear Madam: Yours is ever a Cordial to me, so am I extremely concerned that my Dr. Mrs. Pegy is ill. I earnestly pray my good God to remove all her ailments and preserve so usefull a person. I trust in his Mercy you will yet see Good Days my Dr. Madam, and Im sure had you been with this ffamily as we much wish't when we had the happiness, that I never thought this world could have given of seeing that Excellent glorious Prince it would a been Dr. Mrs. Pegy her perfect cure. His face and person beyond imagination, wants words to express myself of that charming creature possessed of every Virtue, whom I witnessed take horse last Thursday Five in the Evening, left his Palace with his guards and huzzars the rest of the army being gone the day before except Lochyel who went away Friday. This is a melancholy Town, not a highlandman to be seen in it. Soldiers from the Castle has plundered many houses here, Duke Hamilton's, Duke Perth's where they got a valuable Cross, was vastly rude to Lady Lochyel going to murder her. She went to General Guest but got no protection, only they shou'd not come again to her. I saw her last night in young La. Balcies who is not well. Doctor Clare gives her La. medicine ever since she came to Town. I think it's more than time I were telling you I saw your friend frequently, and that day he left the Town both in his house and amongst the Guards of which he was one of, or I had my Dr. Mrs. Pegy whom I assure every of her concerns we always reckons ours. I hope he'll do extremely well, and that the Almighty will bring all things to a blessed ending. Mrs. Sharp came to Town Monday last week was seeing us on Sunday, has been very kind to your friend. Her spirits and many folks is right low just now hearing nothing of our Chief concerns. They all marched from Dalkeith Sunday morning. I look for the best trusting in his boundless Goodness as my Dr. Mrs. Pegy must do the same, and accept with the ffamily of the kind humble service of this my Dr. Madam ever to serve you Adieu.

Edinr. Novr. 6th 1745.

P.S. All of us was very sick in great hazard at sea, but thought we was overpayed with the sight of that lovely person. He came smiling to us, spoke to my Lady asked when she came to Town, claped Archy and said they were pretty Children. We all staid and saw his Royal Highness dine. Everything very grand served in his own silver plate. On his right hand D. of Perth, E. Kelly, Mr. Wm. Murray, Glenronald [Clanranald]. At food Col. Strikland, left hand Lord Geo. Murray, the French Envoy a very pretty man, then Sir Thomas Shiredon [Sheridan].

Memo. From Edinr. to Mrs. Peggy Sharp in St. Andrews very much in favour of the P . . . . . Not signed.

LETTER 56

William Drummond, Viscount Strathallan, who had been 'out' in 1715, joined the Prince at Perth at the beginning of October 1745. Before the Highland army marched south, Strathallan was appointed to command the force gathering at Perth, with Oliphant of Gask as his lieutenant. He was killed at Culloden leading his own troop of horse. His eldest son, James, also 'out' in 1745, was attainted and died abroad in 1765. His wife, Margaret, daughter of the second Lord Nairn, was imprisoned in Edinburgh Castle in February 1746 for her enthusiastic support of the Prince's cause; 'witnesses say they frequently saw her drink the Pretender's health and success to his arms in Britain and said that she put out illuminations on the Pretender's birthday in a most remarkable manner.' She was released on bail in November 1746.

Sir: As I had his Royal Highness the Prince of Wales his Commission as Governor of Perth to raise contributions of such of his subjects as have not joined the Royal Standard, I hereby demand of you to send in to me here for the use of his Royal Highness the sum of Two hundred pounds sterling betwixt and the middle of this Month. As you wish well to his cause I have no doubt of your complying with this desire, and if it shall prove otherwise, I hope you will excuse my executing my orders in a way that will be much more disagreeable to him who is, Sir,

your most humble Servt.
Strathallan.

Perth 6 Novemr. 1745.

Memo. From Lord Strathallan to the Laird of Inchmartin to pay 200 pounds for the use of his Royal Highness.

LETTER 57

This letter was written to John Innes, younger, of Edingight, who is described in Rosebery's *List* as being 'a Rebel Volunteer who when he returned home his Father would not harbour.' He was the eldest son of John and Jean Innes of Edingight, and joined the Highland army as a volunteer. Apparently, although at first after Culloden his father would have nothing to do with him, he became reconciled to him, and he succeeded to the estate in 1750. He was twice Provost of Banff, and died in 1790 while holding the office.

Banff 6th November 1745.

D: B: Yours of the 25 came safe to hand with the accounts of you being made a Cornet and that in your Absence, which is disagreeable to your friends. As to the Horsemen and Armour none here will take any concern in that. If Mr. Hamilton [John Hamilton: see Letter 53] could get you a step higher in the Horse or a Company of foot with liberty to come North to recruit, in either of the above cases I am of opinion that you would be attended with success, and you may depend on my assistance. But without your own Presence nothing can be done. All friends in this Country are in perfect good health. I make offer of my service to Mr. Hamilton and pray let me hear from you both which will be very agreeable.

When you write any letters to this country direct them for your brother Thomas or John Gordon to the care of the Post master of Banff, and they'l come safe to hand but I expect to see yourself soon, as do's the most of your ffriends.

Memo. Letter without a name from Bamff to John Innes younger of Edingreht [Edingight] inclosed under cover to John Hamilton Esqr. of the Palace of Holy Rood house, acquainting him that his friends are not pleased to hear he is made a Cornet but if Mr. Hamilton could get him a higher post in the Horse or a Company of foot with liberty to come to the North to recruit, it might be attended with success.

A letter from a lady, wishing that she had been given the opportunity of kissing the Prince!

My Dear Madam: I had this day the favour of your Letter which I am at a loss in what way to express my gratitude to you for taking so much trouble in writing me such a full and distinct account. I had indeed heard several accounts but none so satisfactory as yours. Your printed paper was exceeding pretty well wrote on and I had not heard of it being in the Country untill I had it from you. I could perceive no mark of being broke up upon your Letter, and I believe they stand as good a chans in the Bag as any way, and as I can assure you that a few lines from you would allways be most obliging were there no news of consequence in the Country, I hope you will continue to be indulgent to me upon those occasions. The Armys marching into England will increase our Curiosity, and you must know a deal more than we can here, so that I will rely upon your Goodness to me from time to time. There shall nothing hinder me from being punctuall in my answers, but the dulness of our Country and the little material we have to put up a Letter. I wish I had it in my power to give you a greater proof of my friendship, I am sure I should loose no opportunity of showing my readiness. If you will be so good as let me know what grounds it is reckon'd by People of most penetration, there is of hopes or fears as to the reception they will meet with in England, and if they have a party in the Parliament or Fleet. I know you have a friend that is as able to . . . from the circumstances of the . . . as any in Edinr.

I cannot blame the Ladys much that oprest the P . . . . . to kiss them for I believe had I been in the Town I would sought one too, and I would have great joy so to do. For I have a great many acquaintances with him that I could have troubled to introduced me. There is no man I am better acquaint with than Lochyel, who I think has made himself as famous as any one in the Army. I shall end with assuring you of Mama's and Sisters

regaird for you, and that and my Complements to your sister, and you may believe me to be my Dr. Madam, your faithful and obliged humble Servt. Adieu.
Wednesday Novr. 6th 1745.

Memo. Letter without a name to Mrs. Forbes of Knapirnie [?] in Mr. Hugh Crawfoord's Lodgings in Edinr.

LETTER 59

Alexander, 6th Earl of Galloway, a landlord in the old Covenanting Country, was naturally a great Whig, though his sister, Lady Margaret Stewart, widow of the Jacobite Lord Southesk, married the Master of Sinclair, son of the Lord Sinclair who had been attainted for his share in the 1715 Rising. Even Murray of Broughton, who involved anyone he could, had to admit that Galloway worked wholeheartedly for the Government.

Strangely enough, long after the '45, his widow—he died at Aix in 1774—became a great friend of the old Jacobite Bishop, Robert Forbes, and his wife. Forbes wrote of her, 'Her ladyship, I believe, means well and has sterling loyalty, which in my estimation is a great virtue.'

Newtown Novemr. 6th 1745.

Dearest Sister: As I have not been four Miles from this place since I wrote to you last, as I'm no body, and I hear from very few, I can have litle to say, further than to let you know that we are all in perfect health, and in present peace and Tranquility. Only we have been alarmed with many lyes and storeys which I did not believe and gave me no pain. We were often told that a party of Highlanders were coming into this Country to raise Contributions from the Burroughs, and to take up Arms and horses. Rich people are easily freighted, Mr. Murray took the alarm, and upon hearing they had been at Douglas visiting the Duke, he expected such a Complement. Upon the 29th of last month he and our sister, with six horse loads of God knows what, went aboard a Port Patrick boat about four miles from their own house and so put to sea. God only knows where they are gone or when they return; when they do they must heartily repent they ever went away. I shall be very glad to know that you and Ld. Sinclair are well, where you intend to pass the winter. My spouse offers her most affectionate Complements to you as we both do to Ld. Sinclair. All your young friends particularly Peggy offer their humble Duty to their Aunt, with the greatest affection friendship and regard I ever am Dearest Sister, yours Gallowaye.

Memo. From Galloway of Newton giving an Accot. of Mr. Murray going off to sea.

LETTER 60

Charles Cumine of Kinninmouth, Aberdeen, owing partly to straitened circumstances, and partly to the persuasions of Lord Pitsligo, joined the Prince at Edinburgh. His wife was the Hon. Sophia, daughter of Lord Forbes, her mother being a sister of Lord Pitsligo. 'Our Uncles cold is still heavy upon him' refers to Pitsligo, who was sixty-seven at this time.

After Culloden, Charles Cumine was in hiding at Altrie, but Sophia brought such influence to bear on George II that she secured pardons both for him and his brother Alexander. She is said to have told King George that it was hard to see her relations loyal to the Crown and she and her children reduced to poverty because 'her husband was a fool.' He died in 1764, having previously handed over the management of his property to his wife.

This letter is written from Floors Castle, home of the Duke of Roxburghe, which is only a mile from Kelso. As the Prince, while at Kelso, stayed at the town house of the Scott-Kerrs, presumably some of the Highlanders were quartered in the castle. The Duke of Roxburghe was a Whig.

My Dearest Life: This is wrote from a Seat of the D. of Rox-brughs, where we have all stayed these two nights, and this day we cross the Tweed. I hope in God the Journey shall be prosperous and that after this Expedition is happily ended, you and I shall meet with pleasure and Joy. I believe we equally long for it. I thought to have wrote you again from Edinr. but we left it the day after I wrote last which was the 30th, I hope you got that Letter. All friends in the Army are well and in good spirits but your Uncles cold is still heavy upon him, he expects the Journey will carry it off. As to the Cause you may hope and trust it will succeed with the Prince who takes all means possible to encourage his men, and surely deserves a throne. My pen you see wont allow a long letter, but you will not measure my regard by that, so God Almighty bless you and my Dr. Children and believe me forever yours,

Chas Cumine.

Floors 6th Novr. 1745.

Memo. From Chas Cumine at Floors to the Honble Mrs. Cumine at Kinemouth [Kinninmouth].

LETTER 61

A long letter mostly on domestic affairs but mentioning Andrew Auchenleck of Kennoway, Fife, of whom Rosebery's *List* has this: 'Joined the Rebells and carried Arms from after the Battle of Preston till dispers't, was in Rebelln 1715. [Whereabouts] Not known.' Unfortunately nothing is known about Auchenleck's eventual fate; he was probably killed.

Clyton [Clayton, Fifeshire]
7th of November 1745.

Dr. Sr: By this I acknowledge the Receipt of yours of the 10th of October and which I suppose you would know I have received by a Letter my Wife write Mrs. Graham a fortnight ago which I hope she received and her Mama is expecting her answer every Day and by it you would know that Mrs. Simpson her Sisters circumstances requires her being with her about the end of the old year at farthest, which I made no doubt she will comply with, and we shall have the pleasure of seeing you both in this Country which we hope you can the more freely do in that the Highland Army are moved from Edinr. Southward. We are all here (blessed be God) in our Ordinary and offer our kind Complements to all with you, and hath had no disturbance from any body since

I wrote you off there having taken what Guns I had with my gray Galloway. Megginch is here just now and hath been in this Country this fortnight past, not judging himself safer at home, and I hear Lundie and Fellon [?] are both in this Country upon the same account tho we have seen neither. As to our neighbour Mr. Imrie of Dunmore was married on Friday last to one Young's Daughter (of St. Andrews, Regent, their Brother to Lady Findall) by whom its said he will get 90,000 marks and I am assured that he is realy better than 30,000 marks, and she is his only Daughter.

Mr. Balfour of Denbogs Children are just now lying of the Small Pox, the eldest Son is recovered. Mrs. Hay at Mugdram who was here about eight days ago lyes in next month. My wife acquainted her that our Corns were all got in good condition accept two three windefall, as all the Corns in this Country are and I hope to hear the like account from you, tho' I was surprized to hear the other day that the Stirling carrier was telling it was not all got in thereabout, and I hear that there is a good deal out betwixt this and Stirling to the next of the Mills of Forth. Our Mercats contrive to be fully as dear as they were. I sold some Bolls of wheat I had over my Lees at 9£ per Boll, and I hear that both Wheat and Oats sells in our Mercats between five and six pound per Boll.

We have no news but whats in the Prints, which I suppose you will now get again, for I have got non for two Months past. I saw a Letter yesterday which gives an Account that there is no fear that Sir Alexr. McDonald or McLeod will give any disturbance to the Government. I hear of none of the Highlandrs in this Country and non in Perth except three hundred or thereabout at Perth. Our neighbour Mr. Auchenleck of Cunaecho [Kennoway] went and joined the Prince's Army about ten days ago, and I hear he is in the Prince's Life Guard. I saw his Sister yesternight. The Country Clash is that he is much in debt, by which I saw this fear increasing. I am yours etc.

Pat. Murray.

Memo. Patk. Murray of Clyton to Da. Graham in Stirling.

LETTER 62

An interesting letter from a sailor to his wife. The John Scot mentioned is probably the John Scott who appears in Rosebery's *List* as 'Sailor. Aberdeen. Carried arms at Falkirk, Inverury, and Culloden; and tho' scarce better than a Boy, was very active in distressing the Inhabitants of Aberdeen, where he is now in prison.'

He served in Moir of Stoneywood's Regiment, pleaded guilty at his trial in October 1746, was sentenced to death, but was reprieved and transported to Antigua in May 1747.

Aberdeen Novemr. 8th 1745.

My Dear: By John Scots information I came by Mr. Livingstone's Letter wch otherways I was like to hear nothing of it. By wch I am glad to find our interest secured. My Dr I think of sailing to morrow morning if moderate weather though the wind should not be fair, and if no better can be done, see to get up your length, being heartily wearyed here. This I send you in case I should not have the opportunity of stoping as I pass. You need not be afraid of French molesting me, who you have so affectionately entertained at Montrose, which I pray may not prove hurtfull to you all. My LandLord and kind LandLady offer you their respects, my humble respects to all our good friends, I am My Dear

Yours while, John Dunbar.

P.S. My Dear: You'l put Mr. Straton in mind about my transport Bill, and a Guinea I advised him of due by Provost Couts, of my Berwick post charges, My Dear adieu, J.D.

Novemr 9th My Dear: I have the Melancholy news to advise you of that our number being decreas'd for last night by ten at night Robt Dorrat I know not how tumbled from the Key at Forie and having the Boat fast ashore could not get to him till he perish'd. I would have been out this morning but hindered to get him buryed. He had the appearance of doing well and am heartily sorry. I design God willing out this night. My Dear while,

Jno Dunbar.

Memo. From John Dunbar at Aberdeen to his wife at Montrose acquainting her he shall sail from thence and call upon her and that he need not fear the French she having used them so well.

LETTER 63

The writer of this letter was Margaret Turner (*née* Farquharson), wife of John Turner of Turnerhall, Aberdeen, and mother of John Turner, younger, who was 'out' in the '45. She is in Rosebery's *List* as 'most active in engaging men for her son and sent several after him to the Highlands.' The authorities, despite these activities, left her alone, and she died in 1754. Her 'young soger Boy,' John, joined the Prince in Edinburgh, went with the army into England, and 'recruited about 20 men for their [the Highland army's] service on that retreat north.' He escaped after Culloden, was excepted from pardon in 1747, but in 1748 a Grand Jury returned an 'ignoramus' verdict, which was, on a second indictment, changed into a True Bill for High Treason. He lay hidden, however, and in 1755, on the death of his father, he entered into possession of the entailed estates. He died at Beaconsfield in 1802.

Dr Sir: I received your kind Letter with great pleasure and return you a great many thanks for your friendship and Trouble. Am glad to hear by my son that you hold out so well and of your Lady, Miss Jeany and my young soger Boy who I hope will give you Joy by his returning home in triumph which I pray God all of them may do. May he preserve them from all dangers and from the hand of their Enemys. Nelly has been pretty well this long time but regrets her being so unlucky to have left Edinr. at this time, but how soon she heard there was a possibility of traveling nothing would keep her so she went away yesterday. I would have sent this by her but they would not give me time. It will be most kind if you'l be so good to let me hear from you and if you get an answer from the Doctor. Am much obliged to your Lady for her trouble, and my Mother writes me she gave John five guins but I have not heard from [him] since. We see by the news they left the Town, God send them all a happy return. Mr. Turner joins me in this kind Complements to your Lady and Miss, as he does to you having a gratefull sense of all your Friendship to his Children, believe me with the utmost esteem

                    Dr Sir
                         your most affect. humble Servant
                              Margaret Farquharson.
Turnerhall Novr. 7th 1745.

Memo. From Margaret Farquharson of Turnerhall to Mr. Alexr. Symes Bookseller in Edinr.

LETTER 64

Captain Alexander Hardy, the writer of this letter, was billeted at Auchinhove, home of Patrick Duguid (see note to Letter 40), after the skirmish at Inverurie in December 1745. Failing to catch Duguid who was in the neighbourhood, his wife and three small children still living at Auchinhove, Hardy burnt down the house one night, mainly out of spite. It makes one hope that he did not receive the money he is here asking from his parents.

Dr Parents: I wrote you 2 or 3 Posts ago about sending me some Money and has received no answer, and as there is no danger by the Highlanders, I expect your return in 10 days with £6 sterling. As I am not sure how soon I'l be obliged to leave this Country I beg and intreat of you that you would send me it up with all the Expedition imaginable, and I shall give you my promise as soon as I am worth money I shall return all that I have got from you with usury. All the news we hear at present is that the Highlanders is decamped from Edinr and is going for the West of England. By all the information I can get he'll be 15,000 strong for there is multitudes joining him every Day. Lord Kelly joined him Octor. 24th with 500 Men upon his own pay, and if the P . . . . . gains he is to pay him, if not he is to lose all. Likewise I shall give you an Accot who has joined him. Stewarts, Camerons, McDonalds, McLauchlans, McGrigors, McKinnons, McLeods, Duke of Perth,

Duke of Athol, Lord Forbes, Ld Pitsligo, Ld Ogilvie, Gordon of Glenbucket, Ld Galloway, Ld Kilmarnock, Ld Elcho, Lord Douglas, Lockart of Carnwath, Sir Jno Gordon of Park, Hay of Ranas, Glengil [Glengyle], Inverlochy, Sir Thomas Hay, Lord Jno Murray of Brucktown [Broughton], Cluny McPherson, Broadabine [Breadalbane], Ld Kelly, Cowbardie [Cromarty?], Lochyl. I have no Account of any English Gentlemen that have joined him as yet, likewise we expect a Battle every Day for Genl Wade was actually at Berwick upon the 1st instant with about 24,000 Men. Likewise we hear that there is levied up in England about 200,000 Men, whether any of them comes to this Battle I can't tell. We hear that there was lying in Dunkell 200,000 sterl. with Artillery and some small arms for the Prince. This is all the news I can mind at present, beging your Complyance to send that money as soon as possible and write me particularly the news that is in your Country. The harvest is quite over here, but the Meal still continues at an shilling per peck. With my kind Complements to yourself and Uncles and all relations and Mr. Garden, James and Willm. Garden and both my Sisters and all acquaintances and I am with great regard

your most Dutifull and affect son

Alexr Hardy.

Auchenhove. Novr. 7th 1745.

Memo. From Alexr. Hardy of Auchenhove to Mr. Alexr. Hardy Mercht. in Kintyre, giving an Account of the Chiefs that have joined the P . . . . .

LETTER 65

The second column, under the Dukes of Atholl and Perth, the Prince and Lord George Murray commanding the first (see Letter 27), came through Peebles and Broughton and arrived at Moffat on 6 November. A sketch of the Duke of Atholl's career appears in the note to Letter 11.

There is no mention of a Peter Seton in the *Lists of Prisoners*, and the name 'Lathrish' cannot be traced. Possibly it is Lathirst, in Fife, which is meant.

Madam: I take this opportunity of a friend of myn returning from this place to acquaint you that I am very happy in being with Duke of Athole, from whom I hourly receive singular marks of his favour, one instance of which is that on the Road last day, he expressed himself thus—Mr. Seton I assure you it is a great satisfaction to me to have along with me the son of honest Lathrish who I always look'd upon as a second Father—The Duke then acquainted me of the care my Father had of his Mother when big with child of him at the revolution, for which his Grace concluded that he was the Instrument of his coming into the world for wch he justly stiled him his second Father. His Grace added that on that and many other regards he had for my Father he look't on himself next to his own Family, in gratitude to regard me.

   I have only time to add that I ever am
    Madam
      your Dutiful Son and Servant
       Peter Seton.
Moffat 7 Novr. 1745.

Memo. From Peter Seton at Moffat to his Mother Lady Lathrish in Kirkcaldy acquainting her he is very civily treated by the Duke of Athole.

LETTER 66

Another letter from Margaret Turner (*née* Farquharson) of Turnerhall about her son John (see Letter 63). Her mother, to whom she is writing, was Helen Farquharson, wife of Alexander Farquharson, writer to the Signet.

My Dear Mother: Yours I had yesterday. I'm extremely fond to hear by Mr. Rose you are so well, and am hopefull by what he says there are no need of fears from the Castle, so you should make yourself easy. I had a letter from my Son eight days ago with a Copy of the same Account, and as I hear its what he could not want being told that every one in his station behov'd to have

laced Cloaths, I assure you I do not grudge nor did I ever know him to put me to unnecessary Charges. Depend upon it his Accounts shall be payed. I am much obliged to you for the present you gave him for which I return you my hearty thanks. God Almighty be his Protector and Defender in all dangers for the greatest happiness of his Father's Family and give him and all of them a safe return in Triumph. Am surprized he would have left his Watch it being a thing so necessary, and thinks where he ventured himself he might have done it all other things being a trifle in comparison. Mr. Rose tells me your thinking long to have Nel, who, had it not been for the uncertainty of traveling would have been with you long since, But now is positive to venture all hazards, she is to set out soon. I thank God she's much recovered but sometimes yet she has fits of vomiting tho' seldom, Makes me afraid to ventur her a Journey at this Season, But Miss Scott and she are both positive. They come the way of Kinghorn and are expecting a pass from Guest to get over the water, which Mrs. Ronald is to send. I have wrote both my aunts and thanked them. Mr. Turner, and Nelly and the Children join in their most humble Duty to you, as we all do in Complements to all friends, and to my Lady Nidsdall. I pray God preserve you and continue your good health, and believe me with the utmost Gratitude and Respect, My Dr Mother
   your most Dutifull and Loving Daughter
    Margaret Farqrson.
Turner hall. Novr. 8th 1745.

Memo. From Margaret Farquharson of Turner hall to her mother Mrs. Farquharson in Edinburgh.

LETTER 67

David Carmichael, the collector mentioned in this letter, is described in Rosebery's *List* as 'of Balmedie, Collr. of the Cess— Collected the Land Tax for the Rebels and voluntarly accepted of that office. Lurking.'

Madam: I have sent enclosed a Letter that was sent here yesternight from Perth. The Express told me it was anent the Cess whereupon I opend it thinking it needless to send to your Ladyship as I had payed the Cess the day before. But finding it was for a Contribution I have sent it. I paid two Quarters Cess and got a Receipt. David Carmichael collects as formerly and has his Books so that the last receipt was not required. Mr. Charles and Miss are very well. The Lads are now driving out the Muck to the Black land and there is one pleugh tilling it as it is mucked. I am with due regard Madam

Your Ladyship's most Obedt. Servt.

Andw Longmoor

Inchmartine 9th Novemr 1745.

Memo. From Andrew Longmoor to Lady Betty Ogilvie acquainting her Ladyship he had a letter last night for a Contribution.

LETTER 68

William Baird of Auchmedden, whom 'Maria' mentions in the following letter as bringing her mail, was 'out' in the '45, though he did not take a very active part, being Deputy-Lieutenant and Governor of Banffshire under Lord Lewis Gordon. He escaped the penalties after Culloden. He was related by marriage to Sir William Gordon of Park's wife, his wife being Anne Duff, daughter of William Duff of Dipple, whose brother was Lord Braco. Sir William's wife was Janet Duff, daughter of Lord Braco (see Letter 34). This would account for the fact that a member of his family was apparently staying at Park. As William had six sons and four daughters, it is probable that 'Maria' was one of his daughters and that she was writing to her sister in Edinburgh.

My Dearest Miss Duff: I had the pleasure of both your Letters one by Auchmedan and another by the last post. I'l assure it give me great pleasure when I received them for I was beginning to think my Dear Miss had deserted me like the rest of my friends, which you may be sure would give me a great deal of pain. You say in your last you saw my Dr. Knight. I'l assure you I could have given my Eyes for the Sight, but that's a thing I need not think on for I need not expect to see him till all these words be done. All I shall say is Lord send them safe to St. James's. As to my riding Cloaths I'l assure I will have none nor anything till such time as our friends be safe at London, for I would have litle heart to weare anything till that time, I would be very incapable of choice just now. I will delay the Cover of my Saddle till such time as I take off all together. I have not been very well for some time past nor I believe will not be well till I hear our friends is all safe. I beg of you my Dear if you see my Knight tell him I wrote you I was quite well and in top Spirits. Poor man he has litle need of any thing to Vex him just now. I am afraid if things has not a better appearance in a short time I'l have but a small chance to see an end of the Work. It were Charity of you to write me often, there is no such things as Letters miscarried now. I shall assure you I have much need of some Comfort, for I believe my Dear may easily judge the destruction of my mind at present. I shall add no more but my Complements to all my friends, you see I hope you'l ever believe me to be your very affectionate and faithfull

Maria

Park. Novr 9th 1745.
P.S. You'l be so good as write me how to direct you, adieu.

Memo. Letter signed Maria at Park to Miss Hariot Duff at Edinburgh wishing their friends may soon come to St. James's.

LETTER 69

Carlisle was taken by the Prince's Army on 17 November 1745. General Wade set out from Newcastle on the 16th, and got as far as Hexham on the 17th, when he heard that Carlisle had fallen. He returned to Newcastle on the 22nd. Lord Lewis Gordon, as has been previously mentioned, had been appointed Lord Lieutenant of Aberdeenshire and Banffshire.

R. D. Sir: I was glad to understand by your last that all your ffamily are well. I thank God I am a great dale better, but am brought very thin. This is the first time I have ventured so far for this two months. Lord Lewis Gordon came to Town yesternight. I cant say what he is to do, but if I get any Account before the Post go away shall write.

All friends in our Country are well and litle Sandy is in very good health. As for news I cant pretend to write you any at present but will expect to hear from you. It seems the P . . . . . . Army have march'd and it is reckon'd they have pass'd Wade. I have not got a night Cape such as you wanted but shall send it as soon as I can find one, being in heast shall only add my Complements to your Wife and all our friends and believe that I ever am My Dr Sir, your affectionate humble Servt

H. G.

Aberdeen November 9th 1745.

P.S. Lord Lewis Gordon has named a Council at Aberdeen, or if they dont accept he is positive to do military Execution. I shall write more fully afterwards.

Memo. From H. G. at Aberdeen to the Revd Mr. Wm Robertson at Dundee acqng him that Lord Lewis Gordon is come to Town etc.

LETTER 70

This letter is apparently written by the daughter of James Hepburn of Keith, described in Rosebery's *List* as of 'Canongate Edinburgh. Carried Arms in the Rebel Life Guards said to be Captain.' His eventual fate is unknown, as he does not appear on the lists of prisoners.

The Tweed was crossed by the Prince's column on 6 November, and Carlisle was entered on the 17th.

Edinburgh November 10th 1745.

Dear Aunt: I need make you no apologys for being so long of answering your last, you know much about yt time every body got some other thing to think of, and any thing I had to say would have been rather troublesome. What makes me trouble you just now is to inform you Mr. Mercer is in very good health, we sent a Council Post after the Army to know some particulars. Papa writes us they had crossed Tweed, was all in great health and spirits. They were to be at Carlisle on Saturday night where the whole Army are to join, as it has been divided in two different parts, because the Country they went through could not provide Meat and Lodging for such a number of men, As they were all together in England, they wont sustain that inconvenience. Where they go after, that is kept Secret. People gives various accounts of the number of the highland Army, but I know the Prince expects to be joined in England. We have pretty certain Authority that the Prince had assurances from his friends there. I would fain recommend to you Dear Aunt, never to believe one word of what you hear. Never was there on Earth so many lyes invented to distract People. They are allways told from undoubted Authority, if you will take their word for it. You will hear I suppose that the English Army is nineteen thousand Men which is by no means the case. The troops thats come from Flanders are not the half of what is represented. There is not one of the Regiments compleat some wants more than the half. The Regiment Roby is in is not coming over I hope, we had a letter from him last day where he says they got no orders yet.

I am afraid you will very seldom hear from Mr. Mercer as the people in the Post Towns wont further a Letter from that Army. There is some of the Clans wifes in Town that will probably get expressed on any extraordinary occasion, I shall be sure to let you know. I hope Grandmama keeps her health, I offer my Duty to her, my Complements to Mr. Irvine, and love to Jamie, I am Dear Aunt, your affectionate Niece and humble Servant.

Kath. Hepburn.

P.S. I hear all the letters are kept up at the Post Office three or four weeks or they be delivered. As they cant read all the Letters they only open the ones to the most suspected persons, and in case there should be any information in the others they dont deliver them till it cant be of no use. So I suppose it will be about Christmass till this comes to your hand. Adieu, My Sisters join me in their Duty to Grandmama and you.

Memo. From Katherine Hepburn at Edinr to Mrs. Mercer in Aberdeen relating to the Rebells. Novr 10th 1745.

LETTER 71

Carlisle was actually summoned to surrender on 10 November, but did not surrender until the 17th.

As far as Edinburgh was concerned, the principal Government officers, who had disappeared on the Prince's approach, returned there in state on 14 November. Judging from the following letter, the Edinburgh ministers were rather braver, and took over their deserted pulpits some nine days after the Prince's departure, and this although he had, as always, been scrupulous in assuring freedom of worship. He even went to the extent of telling a deputation which waited on him that nothing would be said if the ministers prayed for King George (see also Letter 5). Many men in the Highland army were Presbyterians; 'there were none more affectionate and devoted to their ministers.' Their behaviour is well borne out by the following from the *Gentleman's Magazine*, dated from Derby 13 December, while also showing the strange sense of humour of some of the Government supporters:

'But really what did afford me some matter for an unavoidable laughter (tho' my family in this miserable situation (Highlanders being billetted on them)) was to see these desperadoes, from officers to the common men, at their several meals, first pull off their bonnets, and then lift up their eyes in a most solemn manner, and mutter something to themselves, by way of saying grace, as if they had been so many pure primitive Christians.'

Dr Sir: The Army were to be at Carlisle last night and will pass into England it seems without interruption from Wade the reasons of which not known. There is a rumour of landing and rising in England but no certainty, only upon that, matters now seem to depend, for without either of them it seems impossible, for the Army went from this alone to do it, tho' if they meet with any Encouragement hard to know what they may not do.

Wade they say wants to let them enter into the Nett, but its my opinion such an experiment may come to catch a Tartar. Others give out that his men are lately very sickly with a Fux. Till yesterday there was no preaching in the kirks since 15th Sept. Mr. George Wishart had a fine discourse on the 2 first and 3 last verses of the sixtieth psalm.

Some are so curious as to take notice that there is only among them one Gentleman who heard and joined, is the P . . . ce Ch . . . . . ordinancer, and only four that have taken the Oath of Aleg, so that if it succeeds it will be done without the aid of P[ope] or P[retende]r.
Edinr. 11th Novemr 1745.

Memo. Letter from Edinburgh without a name, the Cover tore off acquainting that the Rebells were to be at Carlisle the 10th Novr 1745.

LETTER 72

There is a manuscript note which some years ago was in the possession of a Mr. Erskine of Cardross, quoted in Rosebery's *List*, which runs as follows: 'Mrs. Mathison's house plundered, and the Ds of Perth's in Canongate; Gask's, Cunochies, Strathalans, Sir H. Stirling's, Lady Barrowfield's [Mrs. John Walkinshaw's], Mrs. Gordon's etc.'

The substance of this letter is remarkably like the description of General Hawley's conduct at Mrs. Gordon's house, Aberdeen, after Culloden. He helped himself to most of the household linen and china, together with anything else that took his fancy. The conduct of the English troops from the castle is in striking contrast to that of the Highlanders, who behaved admirably in Edinburgh. There were, of course, those who by wearing the white cockade brought ignominy on it purposely, by plundering. Lord George Murray issued strict orders against these abuses, and some were tried by court martial and shot on Leith Links. Indeed, until the coming of the English, Whig and Jacobite got on remarkably well in Edinburgh, looking on the Rising as political rather than as civil war.

Dear Anne: I got your Letter and am glad you got safe home and found the Children all well. I ashure you it was good to you that ye was gone from this place, for we have had sad doings in this place. The Prince went from the Abby on Thursday the 31st Octor and Friday the first of Novemr the whole of the Highland Army was gone from this place, and on Saturday the Castle Soldiers was sent down on the Town, and on the collour of searching for Arms they have done great damage and plunder. They have destroy'd the appartment the Prince was in, tore down the silk bed he lay in, broke and carried off all the fine gilded Glasses, Cabinets and everything else. They have done the same to the Duke of Perth's Lodging, its entirely ruined. They have visited the Lady Lochyel and used her in the rudest manner calling her Bitch and Whore, and had the impudence to spit in her face. They have given the same treatment to poor Mrs. Taylor and carryed off most of her goods, she has left her house and gone to stay with her friends. Mrs. Mathison in the Bow [Netherbow] is quite ruined. They have taken 70 pounds sterling value of Goods with 8 Guineas in Gold and 14 Shilings money, and beat herself in a severe manner, and much more damage they have done which would be too tedious for me to write. They also went to the infirmary and beat the poor Highlanders, twist about their Arms and Legs that was set after being broke at the late Battle, tore open their wounds so that their shrieks was heard never so far. Your friend Mr. Bisset hearing and seeing all their doings, brought the Pistolls back to me, for he said he could not protect them, and told they had been at his Fathers house in Leith and broke open Chests and took away a very good Gun and Sword. However there at last came a party to my house, and women along with them, and light Candles in their hand. So they have tak'n the Pistols with the Sadle, but the Cutlass is to the for, being under Botles of beer. So at the expense of my Beer which they drank so greedily, the Cutlass is safe. They never called for any thing to drink it in but set the Bottles to their heads, and all the thanks I got for it was that I was a Dam'd Jacobite Bitch, because I refused to send for Brandy to give them to drink. All our neighbours had the same fate. There was a sad uproar in our wynd.

I had almost forgot to tell you your Daughter Pegie is very well. I send inclosed Mr. Aikmans Accompt and Mrs. Mathison's with Mr. Morrison's discharge.

Our news in this place is that Prince Henry with 1500 men is landed in the West of England and that the Highlandmen has taken Carlisle. My Complements to Mr. Cumming yourself and Children, this day I got his Letter by a Gentleman.

Dear Anne Adieu.

Leith Novr 11th 1745.

Memo. From Leith to Mrs. Cumming at Montrose, giving an Account of the Castle Soldiers plundering the Abby etc.

LETTER 73

Lord Strichen, to whom the following is addressed, was a Whig. A letter quoted in W. B. Blaikie's *Origins of the Forty-Five* from Grant of Grant to Lord Loudoun, dated 9 January 1745/6, has the following about Strichen: 'I have just now received the inclosed for Lord Strichin by Mr. Sime Minister of Longmay. My Lord Strichin did all in his Power to save My Friend Lieutenant Grant from being taken Prisoner, even to the hazard of his own Life.' This incident took place at Inverurie on 23 December, when Lord Lewis Gordon completely defeated MacLeod of MacLeod, and forced him to retreat across the Spey.

The Prince's column crossed the Tweed on 6 November, and the night was spent at Jedburgh. He was at Haggiehaugh on the Liddel on the 7th, while the cavalry went by Hawick and Langholm, and they joined his column again on the 8th near Longtown. On the 9th the Prince's column was joined at Newtown of Rockliff by the second column, under the Duke of Atholl, and on the 10th Carlisle was summoned to surrender. 'C of Derwentwater' was the Hon. Charles Ratcliffe, brother of the 3rd Earl of Derwentwater, beheaded in 1716, and *de jure* 4th Earl. Both were grandsons of Charles II and Mrs. Mary Davis. Charles had also been condemned in 1716 but he escaped to France. Coming over, on board the 'Esperance', to Scotland in November 1745, he was captured, and eventually executed. It may be that the Derwentwater mentioned here is the Hon. James Ratcliffe, Charles's son, who although taken and imprisoned in the Tower with his father, was released.

The Lord Justice Clerk, Judges, and Government Officers, returned to Edinburgh in state on 13 November as mentioned previously.

Wales was, unofficially at any rate, strongly Jacobite, but although Sir Watkin Williams-Wynn and his associates plotted for the restoration of the Stuarts, when that House really needed their support they failed to rise to the occasion, either through irresolution, or because they did not receive the signal from Wynn. There are various stories of letters from the Prince and vice versa, fixing a rendezvous for the Welsh contingent, going astray. Charles wrote to his father in Avignon in 1747 that a Mr. Barry, 'sent by Sir Watkin Wynn and Lord Barrymore to assure me . . . that they were ready to join me in what manner I pleased,' arrived at Derby two days after he had started his retreat.

My Lord: On Wednesday last the Prince past the Tweed with his Division and Guards, and march'd in towards Milnford Green, and when reconnoitring the Ground there, sent orders to Wooller to provide Quarters for 3000 foot and 1000 Horse. Upon which two Regiments of Dragoons and the remains of Hamilton's and Gardners took the flight and never halted untill they were at Newcastle. This alarm'd the whole Army upon which they all retired to Newcastle and stood under Arms all Thursday and that Night. The Prince returned to Jedburgh and from that to Hawick, Longholm, Longtown and Carlyle, which he entered we think yesterday. The advanced Guard as we are informed by servants returned with Carts and Horses, entered Carlyle Thursday last, under the D: of Perths command, and they say were received with Bonfirs and Ringin of Bells. Lord Geo. Murray with the Artillery etc. they say entered Carlyle on Friday and further add that the Duke of Perth was joined by 3000 horses under the Command of C. of Derwentwater. They say Genl

112

Wade returns the road he came by Doncaster so that the High-landers can have no Interruption from their getting into Wales amongst their friends, and some think they will not halt untill they get to London, but send Expresses to their friends to meet them on the Road, for its impossible Wade can reach them as his men are terribly fatigued first with their work in Flanders a Long Voyage and traveling down in very bad roads, For it seems they had great rains in England. The news from London this day say that seven more Regiments are come from Flanders, but at the same time the Gazette takes notice of great Embarkations at Dunkirk etc. from which I am afraid of a landing already. Our prime Ministers (except Lord Advocate) are all returned to their several Houses in the Country. We believe in this Town the session will meet immediately if a sufficient number can be con-vened, and I can see no application as yet to Parliat for any adjournment of the Session, and therefore believe the army will think of moving this way. I'l give you no further trouble untill I hear further from the great folks, some of which I hear are to be in Town tomorrow, this with my Dutifull respects.

Memo. From Edinr without a name to the Lord Strichen near Peterhead acquainting him that the highland army is march'd thro' Carlyle towards Wales Novr 11th.

LETTER 74

At the Council at Derby which voted for retreat, David Morgan, a Welshman and a barrister called 'the Prince's Counsellor,' advised a march into Wales, but his advice was not taken.

Colonel James Innes is in Rosebery's *List* as 'Overseer of the highways of Cullen. Aid du Camp to Ld Ogilvie threatened the Officer of Excise when doing his duty; he was in the Rebellion Anno 1715. Prisoner at Aberdeen.' He had been made a Colonel by the Prince at Edinburgh. Taken prisoner, he was tried at Carlisle in August 1746, sentenced to death, and executed at Brampton in October.

Dr Sir: I had yours of the 4th Current this day, but sometime ago I sent you under Cover of Mr. Adam Duff all the papers that were publish'd here at that time, which you have no doubt received before now and I herewith send you two others that have come abroad since. But you need not expect any more on that side of the question for some time at least because the Scene is now changed since the Army went from this place which was upon Friday the first of this Month.

I saw Coll Innes at Inveresk upon Saturday after, he had been for some time in the West Country upon a Party levying Cess etc., and was like to have been roughly handled by the Whiggs in that Country, however he escaped without any hurt. We are much in the Dark here about the motions of either of the Armys. Many storys are told of a landing in favours of the Prince, but as yet without any Certainty. Its generally believed that as the Prince is just now far Inferior to Genl Wade in numbers, his design is to penetrate into the West of England as far as Wales, where they expect to be joined by numbers in that Country, but whether this can be done, I'm not acquaint with the Situation of the Country so well as to judge. I refer you to the mercury inclosed and am Dr Sir,

Your most humble servant
Thos Riddock.

Edinr. 11th Nov. 1745.

Memo. From Thomas Riddock of Edinr to Wm Leslie of Melrose Esqr at Banff with an Account that it is believed the Rebells are marched to the West.

LETTER 75

From the contents of the next letter it is quite obvious that even though he was 'pressed' into the Prince's service, the writer was rather an unpleasant individual. Apparently, until he became ill, he was in Lord Ogilvy's Regiment, but he is not the Alexander Smith, also of Arbroath, who turned King's Evidence against Major

Nicholas Glascoe, as that gentleman was taken at Culloden, and the writer of this letter ended up in Edinburgh. 'Shand Crighton' may be James Crichton of Arbroath, who was in Ogilvy's Regiment, and was transported in March 1747.

'Lieutent Watson' was probably John Watson, of Ogilvy's, a brewer of Arbroath, who was taken at Culloden, but of whom nothing further is heard, and 'Lieutent Mudy' may be David Mudie, of Glamis, of Ogilvy's, who was liberated in April 1747, having been captured at Glamis shortly after Culloden.

'The Doctor of the Regiment' was Thomas Crighton of Dundee, of whom it is recorded in Rosebery's *List* that he 'acted as Surgeon, joined after Preston and carried Arms with the Rebels till after Culloden. Near Blair Gowery. Lurkg.' It is not known what eventually happened to him, as he is not mentioned in any other list.

'Sergeant Beard' was William Beard, a collier of Falkirk. He was tried at Carlisle in September 1746, sentenced to death, but reprieved and ordered to be transported. He was eventually pardoned on condition he enlisted in the regular Government forces.

'David Gray' was a weaver of Arbroath, and was taken on suspicion in July 1746. He was probably the David Gray who turned King's Evidence against Lord Balmerino.

Edinburgh Novemr 12th 1745.

Loving Wife: This is to let you know that I am living that is all. I arrived here yesterday. I have been very badly used since I saw you: Shand Crighton and us came into Edinr upon the fifth of this month and as we came along the Bridge of Leith the Generall was beating for to march to Dalkeith which we was obliged for to go with the rest. We was not two hours there when the Duke of Perth give orders for to march to a part called Lonhead where we lay all night in a park all night six miles from Dalkeith. Tomorrow we went to a part called PennyCook, where we lay in a Barn about five hundred of us, and not one sheaf of straw to one of us. And from that to Peebles, where walked the Streets the whole night and upon the Morrow was obliged to take the Drum, and I bear till I sweat and trembled for perfect hunger, and we was obliged to travel twelve miles before we halted to a part called Moffat, and we camped upon the plain we got every man one Bisket. Tomorrow we went within six miles of Carlysle, where I took a fever and lay there five Days in a kiln, where I had no friend there byt Lieutent Watson and Lieutent Mudy. They brought the Doctor of the Regiment and he drew Blood of me twice in less than one hour's time, and all the Cordial was for me a bit of burnt Bread in a litle water for twenty four hours time. And when they went away Sergeant Beard give me two shilings and told me that was all he got for me, But they would not leave nobody. Then when recovering of my health, my thighs and Legs swelled as big as my Waste which still continues. I cannot go three times through the door but I must sit down. The minister of Tweedhill upon Tweed sent a Man and a horse with me to Dalkeith, and my Aunts son came with a horse for me to Edinr. I had not one thread upon me when I came but an old walop I got from Alexander Ramsay that was with David Gray, my Razours and my hone. They stold my plaid the second day we went from Dalkeith. A great deal of my Lord Ogilvie's men has not a shift to put on. As for myself I put on my three shirts all together and they never came off till I came to my Aunt's house. So I have no more to trouble you at present but my Duty to my Babes and all my friends and I will see them as soon as possible.

Alexr Smith.

I am able to walk. My aunt and her son has their service and would be glad to hear of you well being.

Memo. Alexr Smith at Edinr to [Mrs.] Alexr Smith at Arbroth giving an Accot of the Highland Armys March.

LETTER 76

It would seem that the French man-of-war lying off Stonehaven, and mentioned in the next letter, was the advance guard of Lord John Drummond's force which landed at Montrose, Stonehaven, and Peterhead on 22 November (see note to Letters 28 and 29). This particular man-of-war does not seem to be mentioned in any of the contemporary accounts. It may be the ship from which were taken the cannon used to capture the 'Hazard' (see Letter 82).

Dr Brother: I received yours dated the 7th current wch gives me satisfaction and am exceeding glad to hear of your welfare as your Mother and we all are in good health only times extraordinary troublesome here. We have a man of war lying before our Town daily expecting it to be battered to the Ground, which breeds no litle stir, as we have 40 or 50 Men on guard every night. For by the French men that is here, which I heartily wish we were quite of, so we have been in great confusion ever since the highland Army came to Perth. I am very glad that you and your Master has agreed let me know your terms, but I remember you write me that you have referred it to him. Let me know how you and your neighbour does agree and the situation you stand in with respect to insight and learning which I am hopefull you'l not neglect. I had not mind when you agreed with your Master to desire the favour to have a 14 days liberty about Christmass, but I expect you'l get that from him, or let me know and I shall write him to free you that time as I will expect you to write me in Course fully how you are. Pray be carefull to your masters interest as you are a Stranger, and everyone is ready to look, so I entreat you'l not neglect it. As times is but very indifferent, I shall allways be glad to hear from you and let me know what you have need of which you know I will endeavour to transmit you. I am in great heast wishing God may preserve you from all trouble and Evil, so let me know in Course and we are yours affectionately
                                        Alexr Robertson.
Stonehaven the 12th Novr 1745.

P.S. I would a write you sooner but we are allways in a hurrie. Cargill is going of from us ye 6th Febr next.

Memo. From Alexr Robertson at Stonehaven to his bror at Edinr acqg him there is a man of war there, and that they have a Guard of 50 Frenchmen.

The total ration strength of the Prince's army which marched to Derby was 7587, though it is not possible to say how many camp-followers were included in this number. It was composed as follows:

Cavalry

Lord Elcho's Life Guards	125
Lord Balmerino's Life Guards	40
Lord Kilmarnock's Horse Guards	100
Pitsligo's Horse	120
Huzzars under Baggot	70

Infantry

Lochiel's Regiment	740
Appin's Regiment	360
Athole Brigade (3 battalions)	1000
Clanranald's Regiment	300
Keppoch's Regiment	400
Glencoe's Regiment	200
Glenbucket's Regiment	427
Ogilvy's Regiment	500
Perth's Regiment	750
Robertson's Regiment	200
Maclachan's Regiment	260
Glencarnock's Regiment	300
Nairn's Regiment	200
Stewart's Regiment	450
Various Units Regiment	1000
	7542

Artillery

Commanded by Colonel James Grant a French officer.

1 unmounted iron gun carried in a cart drawn by a pony.

6 Swedish field-guns, 2- to 4-pounders from France, with French gunners.

6 1½-pounders, captured from Cope at Prestonpans.

Unfortunately there was no truth in the story of a rising or a landing in the West of England (see Letter 73).

Dear Sir: I had yours of the 30th ulto and would have answered it sooner had I had any thing worth writing, and tho' I have still little to write worthy perusal, yet I hope it will force another from you which will be allways most agreeable. I was yesterday waiting of a Gentleman lately come from Edinr who as I understand is one appointed for levying the Publick Taxes, but in what manner I cannot inform you, he being only to meet this day at Aberdeen with some others to concert methods. He ashures me the P . . . ces army was full 12,000 strong when he left Edinr besides severall more from the North who were hourly expected, and that there were the strongest ashurances of his being joined by considerable numbers of the English how soon he appeared amongst them. And that there would be a landing in the west of England by the time he came there, so that in all human Probability our civil wars would soon be ended in the most advantageous way for our Country, which all true lovers of it must sincerely wish. Lord Loudon [*sic*] is still at Inverness recruiting but with no great success not having got above three hundred men as yet. This is all I hear at present, how soon any thing worth noticing occurs shall acquaint you. My best wishes to my niece and your young folks, and I hope you'l believe that I most sincerely am

My Dr Sir yours etc. E. F.

Bamff 12th Novr 1745.

Memo. From E. F. at Bamff to Mr. John Auchterlony in Montrose acquating him that the P . . . . . . Army is 12,000 strong, and that there was a landing in the west of England etc.

LETTER 78

Lord Lewis Gordon was, of course, the Prince's Lord Lieutenant in Aberdeenshire and Banffshire.

Lord Loudoun, who had fled with his regiment and Cope after Prestonpans, returned to Inverness on 11 October. The *London Gazette*, 26–29 October, has this:

'Whitehall, October 29. By Letters from Inverness of the 11th and 12th every Thing was very quiet in that Part of the country. The Earl of Loudon arrived there on the 11th, in order to take upon him the Command of the Troops in those Parts, and of the twenty new Independent Companies raising there, under the Direction of the Lord President of the Session [Lord President Forbes], which were in great Forwardness, and would, in all probability, soon be compleated.'

On 16 August Forbes had gone to Inverness and brought in for the Government the Lords Sutherland and Reay, the Grants of Grant, the Munros and others.

Dr Sir: I reckon by the time this comes to hand, the maid servant I engaged for my Sister will be with you. As for the Boy I spoke to some time ago and who seemed willing to engage at that time notwithstanding all the enquirys I have made, I can get no accounts of him. I have wrote this day to his Father and desired he may get notice of him and cause him speak to me. I have little or no news to entertain you with. Our Ld Lieutenant is recruiting very successfully as is Ld Loudon about Inverness tho' not with equal success, he not having raised above 400 Men most Munroes and Sutherlands not a very formidable sett. There are some Gentlemen appointed in this Country for levying the publick Money, but in what manner it is to be done I cannot as yet inform you as they were only to meet at Abdn on Monday last to concert the Method. If there is anything remarkable in your Country I beg you'l acquaint me, as you may expect to be of what happens here worth writing. As Business of all kind is quite at a stand here, I have some thoughts of passing the tedious winter Evenings with you at Guynd, where if I should not make the Expences of the Campaign at Picquet, I shall at least live on the Enemys ground in free quarters.

Write me if there are any accounts of Pourie or Inchmartin, my best wishes to my Sister and your Janiparys and I most sincerely am, Dr Gundy yours etc. C. F.
Banff 13th Novr 1745.

Memo. From C. F. Banff to John Auchterlony Esqr of Guynd acqng that the Lord Lieutent was very successful in recruiting.

A good deal of the gossip in the following letter was false. The Mackintoshes and the Frazers did not join the Prince until December at Glasgow, the Mackintoshes under Lady Anne Mackintosh, and the Frazers under the Master of Lovat. The Earl of Cromarty also, although he received a summons from the Prince written from Borradale on 8 August, did not join him until Glasgow. Lord Fortrose had brought his Mackenzies in to join Lord Loudoun's Regiment in August, men who would otherwise have joined the Prince.

Malcolm Ross of Pitcalny held a commission in Loudoun's Regiment, while Roderick Chisholm of Strathglass, although specially excluded from the Act of Indemnity, apparently did not take an active part in the Rising. The Chisholms were led by his youngest son, Roderick Og, who 'headed about eighty of the Chisholms at the Battle of Culloden himself and thirty thereof were killed upon the field.' Three of his brothers fought on the Government side under Cumberland at Culloden, and a fourth, a doctor at Inverness, took no part.

No man was more feared or hated in the Prince's army than Coll MacDonell of Barisdale, but presumably because he did not know his character, or perhaps did not want to lose his aid, the Prince made him a colonel and gave his son Archibald a major's commission in August 1745. Coll joined the Prince at Aberchalder on 27 August with men he had raised in Knoydart. After Prestonpans he returned home and raised some 300 more men, mostly Mackenzies, and with these he joined the Prince again at Bannockburn in January 1746 and was present at Falkirk. He was too late for Culloden, having been attempting to reduce Ross and Sutherland, and he then made terms with the Government to betray the Prince. He was fortunately unable to do this, was discovered in his treachery, bundled aboard the Prince's ship which took him to France in September, and imprisoned him there until 1749 on a charge of treason. He eventually died in Edinburgh Castle in 1750.

Elgin 13th Novemr 1745.

Sir: The Body of Men passed the Forth since the March of the Highland Army has probably been the McIntoshes (not the Frazers) and other recruits, since am informed there was about

1500 Men about that time at Perth. Its certain the E—— of Cromarty marched Monday the 4th inst with a Body of his own Men and other recruits especially Mackenzies that have gone. Whether Fortrose would or not, credibly reported to be 500 Men, and it seems the Frazers have at last marched with a Body said to be 800 headed by the Master of Lovat, tho' its thought Lovat must have picked up a good many recruits besides Frazers to make out that number. Ross of Pilcanie [Pitcalny], Chisholm of Strathglas's Men have joined this Body as has McDonald of Barrosdale [*sic*] with 4 or 500 McDonalds and Mc-Clains [*sic*] etc. picked up by him. In a word Barrosdale writes from Delphinie [Dalwhinnie?] that they were all that length in their way to join the Highland Army and reckons up the different Corps to the number of 2950 Men.

There's a Company of the McKays [*sic*], one of the Sutherlands, and one of the Munroes, one of the McHannish [*sic*] his men, and at least one of the Grants joined Ld Loudon as its said both the Companys of McKlelans [*sic*] and that of McDonalds have done. But its doubted if these men will stay as they are indorsed to other leaders than their respective Chiefs, and few think they would draw a Sword against the Highland Army or their adherents, tho' they do stay with Loudon. But its certain they desert every day and confidentily reported that last week a great number went of in a Body and carried ten McKlelans that guarded the Bridge that night (to prevent Desertion) along with them with Arms and all accoutrements to join as its said the highland army. We hear of a French ship arrived at the Isle of Man and that the inhabitants of the adjacent Countrys exerted up Arms, Ammunition and Money by way of volunteering, as there was no other party at hand. Lord Fortrose its reported cannot prevail with his men to make up his two companys for Lord Loudon.

Memo. Letter not signed from Elgin to Mr. Alexr Robertson writer to the Signet at Edinr giving an account that the Body of Men passed the Forth was McIntosh's.

The Highland army was at Brampton, awaiting the surrender of Carlisle, from 11 to 16 November.

The writer of this letter was the Reverend Robert Lyon, incumbent of the Episcopal Church in Perth, Chaplain to Lord Ogilvy's Regiment, and he is writing to his sister, Cecilia Lyon. He joined the Prince at Perth, and served throughout the campaign at his own expense. Although as a chaplain he never bore arms, he was found guilty of treason, and sentenced to death at Carlisle. In his last speech he forgave his denunciation by George Miller, town clerk of Perth:

'But in Obedience to the precept, and after the divine example of my blessed Master, Jesus Christ, I heartily and cheerfully forgive them, as I do all my adversaries of whatever kind, particularly George Miller, Clerk of Perth, who, I have reason to believe, has prosecute me to death, and whom to my knowledge I never injured in thought, word or deed. Lord grant him repentance that he may find forgiveness of God. And more especially I forgive the Elector of Hanover by virtue of whose unlawfull commission I am brought to this violent and publick death, and whom I consider as my greatest enemy, because he is the enemy of my holy mother, the Church, of my King, and of my Country.'

The Reverend Robert Lyon, who administered the sacrament to a large number of condemned men, including Thomas Coppoch the teacher of Manchester Grammar School whom Prince Charles made Bishop of Carlisle, before their executions, himself suffered death at Penrith on 28 October 1746. He behaved 'upon the scaffold, with the same calmness and composure of mind and the same decency of behaviour, as if he had been only a witness of the fatal scene.'

Dear Cicie: I take this opportunity of writing by an occasion to Edinr and I hope it shall come safe to hand. The greatest Body of our Army came to this place Monday last and have rested here till now. How much longer we will continue here I know not. All as yet goes well, and all your friends and acquaintances are in good health and in full Spirits. Coud I command so much time I would have writen to Mr. Ramsay and Mr. Aberneathie to put them in mind of taking care of my people in my absence that they may not want Worship, but I hope this they will be diligent in providing without repeated Admonitions.

In the meantime you may cause write to my Cousin David Lyon, whom I hear is not in Deacons orders, to stay at Perth that he may supply for the weekly prayers at least, and on Sundays if they should not have a Presbyter. Make my Complements to all my friends in General with you, and in Least I am as ever Dr Cicie

Yours etc. R. L.

Brampton, 7 miles South East of Carlisle 13 Novr 1745.

P.S. If you meet with any Body going to the Army write me your news and direct it to me in Lord Ogilvy's Regiment and it will come to hand.

Memo. Letter from R. L. in Lord Ogilvy's Regiment to Mrs. Cecilia Lyon at Perth relating to the Rebell Army.

LETTER 81

The Government forces, both naval and military, did their best always to terrorise the inhabitants of any part of Scotland which came under their control. It was policy 'from the highest level' that the rebellion must be stamped out ruthlessly.

Early in November, the 'Hazard' sloop, of sixteen guns and with a crew of some eighty men, commander Captain Hill, came into the harbour of Montrose and anchored, with the result described in the next letter.

John: The present melancholy state of the Country must intercept all correspondence, has kept me several times from writing and it seems has the same effect on you and all others for I have been without hearing from you or any other at Edinr these several posts without so much as the news prints. There lyes in the Harbour of Montrose the Hazard sloop who orders (I mean the Capt) the packett to be brought him without delivering out any Letters. I know not by whose orders he acts, if I knew who it was and had access to him I would certainly complain of this Capt's

conduct who I'm sure with his crew do's more hurt to the Government than the like number of men in Arms against it can do. He has burnt down two ships and unrigged the whole, on Sunday night fired several loaded Cannon upon the Town and has obliged most part of the inhabitants with their ffamilys to fly the Town, and threatens to burn all the fishing Boats, that the poor people tho' innocent are in a miserable state, and both Town and Country here are much to be pityed. On the one hand the Highlanders when there is occasion for it force the inhabitants to serve them, who being without the protection of the Government must comply. Then upon sending this ship, in place of giving relief comes upon an errand to hurt and destroy. Since I know not before whom to lay this Just grievance, I open it that you take occasion of telling it to all such as may have it in their power to put a stop to it. Our present confusions it seems has also put a stop to all Business. I've not as yet heard if the transaction of that affair with Coln Cochrane goes on and if the disposition to him is in a finishing way. I should be glad to hear of Grange where he is and what doing and of that ffamily in England. We hear that our Banks are again opened, if so will I get payment of Midsummer's Salary, upon payments put into the old Bank? Amongst other storys here ther's no money in Specie, nor are Bank notes Currant.
Dun 14th November 1745.

I'm just informed that this Capt yesternight apprehended 3 or 4 Gentlemen, one of them the Minister of Menmure, kept them Prisoners all Night aboard of his ship. One of them is put and keept in Irons because having a publick house he lodged some of the Highlanders tho' it was not safe to refuse them. This shoud have gone by the way of Montrose by Thursdays post, but durst not riske it, therefore sende it this day being the 16th to Arbroth and at the same time have wrote Ad Byng and Genl Guest complaining of this Sloop that there is no need for you to have them addressed. You'l take care to have the enclosed forwarded to Mr. Arbuthnot, its about the Sloop and perhaps he may have some influence. Mrs. Erskine desires you'l with the next post send some few pounds of fresh new hopps, so many as he can conveniently carry, and since the Capt. of this Sloop intercepts the Packett, say then wont my news print? Send it by the post Boy to be left at Kennedys the publick house at Montrose, or at Dunsmalone if he comes that way.

Memo. Letter without a name from Dun to Mr. John Thomson writer in Edinr complaining of Capt. Hill of the Hazard.

LETTER 82

The Jacobites at Montrose determined to get rid of the 'Hazard,' and the following letter, from a supporter of the Government to Hill, was an attempt to wreck the plan. The attempt, however, failed because with Major Nicholas Glascoe of Dillon's Regiment in charge of the battery on Dial Hill, which consisted of the cannon from Perth and two 9-pounders from one of Lord John Drummond's French ships, and with the assistance of Captains Erskine and Ferriers of Ogilvy's Regiment and a party of men (see note to Letters 28 and 29), the 'Hazard' was captured on 24 November. She was fitted out, renamed the 'Prince Charles,' and sent to France for money and stores. Unfortunately on the 25 March, returning from France with some £12,000 and stores on board, she was pursued by four English ships and forced aground at Tongue in Lord Reay's country. Her money, stores and crew were taken, and Lord Cromarty and his son, with others sent from Inverness to try to recapture the money, were also made prisoners.

Sir: You know I was with you on the 13 inst. Since that time I have heard of a plot by the Highlanders which I thought fitt to advise you of. Not that I need to put you on your guard, but to inform you of the places where they are proposing to make attacks. They have sent to Perth for four piece of the Cannon that came from France, and they propose to make Batterys on the Inch that lyes bewest your ship, and at the Back of a Sandy Brea opposite where your ship lyes. All this they propose to do in the night time, but whether the Stormy weather and peoples advice will prevent them I know not. There arrived here this day a small sloop with a Lieutent from the Admirals ship, and fifteen other Men who are disrigging all our Vessels. When they came before, Capt. Wallace called his Guard and was to stop their coming, but our Provost was to raise the whole inhabitants. Whereupon the great Captain went out of Town and all his Guard lay'd down their Arms. There is still more Captains arising here, there is no less than three, Capt Wallace, Captain Gray Pearson and Capt Mill. If you thought proper I should give you a List of all the persons here who hath lifted Arms against the Government, hopeing you'l Excuse this freedom, I am with due regard, Sir,

Your most obedt humble servt
James Fauld.

Arbroath Novr 16th 1745.

That you may understand the paper I left with you, this is a Copy of the Letter to which it is an answr.

Gentlemen: This serves to acquaint you that there is just now an Express come to our famous Captain showing that there is another French Ship off Montrose. There has been several Boats at her but they cannot take her in at present on account of the Storm, so you will be carefull to acquaint the Men of War in the Firth. You know I sent you an Express when the last vessell landed at Stonehaven, I hear this Ship is loaded with Arms, Ammunition etc. As to morrow is the King's Birthday we are in a strait how to get it observed by making any publick appearance, being threatened by the Captain and the strong guard that he has got raised here, that if any shall put illuminations in there windows there houses is to be fired.

Signed only J. F.

and sent to Messrs. George Mudie and George Lyon Merchants in Dundee.

Backt only G. M.

Memo. From James Fauld of Arbroath to Capt Hill of the Hazard acquainting him of the Rebells intentions to raise a Battery in the night and that they had sent to Perth for four pieces of Cannon.

A pleasant letter, though the writer appears to be of the Whiggish persuasion.

November 24th 10 at Night.

My Dr Jeany: In my last I wrote you of John Spittle's illness, since which time he has contrived worse and worse, till this day we have the agreeable news of his having sleept a good deal last night and his pulse is not near so much sunk as it has been for some days past, so there is still some hopes of his recovery. It is a fever not Comon, for tho' he raved so much it was all they could do to keep him in Bed, his pulse was quite sunk at the same time. Poor France Drummond is dangerously ill of a pluratick fever. My Dr. Jeany I have wrote you a number of Letters of late I am certain you have not got, but it gives me no trouble to write them and I have the pleasure to think that they that gets them will have a great deal to read them for besides nonsense with which my epistles abound I am a great proficient in spelling ill. These two accomplishments I look'd on as horrible defects till now. I am not at liberty to write you the news or rather the lyes of this Town so I have only now to beg you'l offer the Complements of all this ffamily to your Mama and the Gentlemen on the Straw, as you name the prisoners, but I by no means think you stile proper. I ashure you the Gentlemens healths is remembered in general next the King in this house, and a great many in particular. We have a good many Cockades here every day but they by no means make us forget our old friends. I have no more to say at present but begs if this comes to hand you'l let me know how all goes at Perth. I am yours, adieu.

Papa is not come home yet.

Memo. To Miss Jeany Scraw at the Custom House, Perth.

Another letter from the rather unpleasant character who wrote Letter 82, enclosing another from a friend. The English army recalled from Flanders began to arrive in London on 23 September, and continued coming over in batches until 1 December. Troops were also landed at Newcastle and Berwick. The *London Gazette* reports on 28 October:

> 'By a Messenger arrived yesterday, who left Marshal Wade, with the Forces under his Command at Darlington on the 26th instant, we have an Account that all the Troops from Flanders were arrived at Newcastle, Berwick, and Holy-Island, except five Companies of Colonel Ligonier's, and three of Brigadier Price's, the Baggage of the Whole, and one ship with Horses, which were still missing.'

It is probably these arrivals to which Fauld's correspondent refers.

I received yours and shoed it to our Magistrate who forwarded it by Express directly to the Kings Ships in the Firth. They are hopefull they may meet with the Vessell before she can get to your Coast. There is just now an Express come to Town bearing Account of General Wade with Eighteen thousand men was landed at Dunbar with a Fine Train of Artillery so that we are very hopefull to have good Accounts of his Expedition very soon. We are begun to solemnize the King's Birthday by displaying our Flags on our Steeple head and in different parts of our Town. I am not sure but I dont doubt our Magistrates will mount the Cross in the ordinary way. As to what you may do I cannot advise you as you have a jealous Governour in your Town, but I am hopefull his Reign shall not be long. Being in heast this is all from yours etc. If I shall get any other good news I shall forward it directly and if you shall hear of the Consequence of the King's Ship meeting with that on your Coast, let me know.

This letter was brought to me at Montrose Novemr 13th 1745 from Arbroth by the person who I have made sign as a contribution to the truth hereof, who says he is a Merchant in the Town of Arbroth, in answer to a Letter sent to Barry Lyon of Dundee dated Octr 9th last.

James Fauld.

Another letter from Margaret Farquharson (*née* Turner) to her 'young soger Boy' (see Letter 63) and one from his father, John Turner.

Turnerhall is in the parish of Ellon, Aberdeen. The parents seem very agitated that he has accepted the post of Quartermaster. This appointment may have been unpleasant in the 18th century, but today it is as good as any other in a regiment. Nelly evidently had her way (see Letter 66).

My dear John: I received two of yours one with the Accounts which shall be payed, another with the Accounts of your March, but as I am informed the Troops is to be some time at Musleburgh so beg you will not fail to write. I want to know by whose advice you accepted of being Quarter Master as I believe your to take no pay. As you are young and cannot be supposed to have experience its not below you to ask advice, and sure I am you have people they are very capable to do it, and would not refuse. My Dear for Gods sake do nothing of moment of yourself for if those Gentlemen to whom I recommended you see you head strong, and not ask them, they will Neglect their promise to me. I am extremely surprized to hear you have never been particularly introduced to the Prince or any man of distinction altho your Grandmama did you to Lady Nidsdeall who promised to get it done next day where you did not go. Its a thing so material it vexes me to the heart you should have neglected it, as you have now lost so fine an opportunity which you hardly can recall. Lay aside that foolish bashfulness and what you think keep to yourself as rash speaking does no Service but gets people Enemys. There is one thing I seriously recommend to you, that is to mend your Duty to Almighty God, who be sure put up your petitions to. I trust in his Mercy he will take care of you and preserve you in all dangers and difficultys, may he of his infinite Goodness and Mercy give you all Victory and send you all home in Triumph is the earnest prayers of your most loving Mother while, Margaret Farqrson.

Am fond to hear all your friends mended you with a litle
money the rest I leave to Nelly who's the Bearer. My Dear.

My Dear Johnie: Your Account shall be duly payed nor do I
grudge it, but am surprized your accepting being Quarter Master.
Who ever advised you to it were not your friends, but since you
have done it acquit yourself well. I'm also vexed you should have
left your watch, and if you have an opportunity gett her, for she
may be ventured where you are. Write frequently for your
Letters will come daily by the Ellon Bag. Lord bless and preserve
you to your affectionate Father, John Turner.

I see by your Grandmother's to your Mama you have goten
Gold from Mr. Hay, let me know how much. Adieu.

Memo. From Margaret Farqrson and John Turner Esqr of Turner
hall to the care of Mr. Alexr Symes in Edinburgh. No date.

LETTER 87

The writer of the next letter was unfortunately very wrong about
the Earl Marischal's landing (see note to Letter 34).

This is Jeany's Birthday
many may she have.
My dear Willy: I wrote to Jeany I had no letter for three Posts,
but I got two in one which unled the Mystery. I am not so afraid
of a Battle as I was now that I hear we have such a great army as
Papa says glorious fellows. I am sure you and all your ffamily
have a light heart now that you are relieved from your Post. I
am sorry the Grays are come down, poor Mrs C will be dreadfull
fear'd. I am just now at Ranchillor and Mama is at home. We
are all very heartsome, we sit up every night very late, and gets
a play of some kind or other.

Mr. McGill grows better every day. We hear that Lord Marshall is landed in the North with 20,000 Men but you need believe

this part of my news no more than you did the rest. You have taken up what I said in my Letter about being angry wrong. I only said I was angry at a certain thing about you, but not at you. No, my D. W. I am not in the least angry at you, this would be an ill time to show it tho I were, when you are so good as write me so often.

Upon further reflection I am not to write you it, I will rather refer telling you it or I have the happiness of seeing you which I hope shall be soon. When I said I would write it you, I was just in the heat of my wrath, but now it is turned to calm resentment. You need not enclose the news papers as we have got them these two or three posts as we used to do. You will excuse my not writing sooner but I could not get an oportunity to send it to Coupar. As I am sure the Servant is waiting for the Letter, so I must end with ashuring you once more I am your most Devoted humble servt

Tilly.

P.S. The paper shall be returned next post but just now it is at Melvil. I wish you would enclose me a French wire as I have not one almost.

Memo. From Tilly to Miss Willy Nisbet at Mr. Campbell's house, Edinr no date.

LETTER 88

A rather agitated fragment, but whether from a Jacobite lady or a Whig it is impossible to say.

My Dear: I beg whenever you hear of the decisive stroke being given, send over Will that Moment which will oblige many here. Your bairns and I is well. Adieu.

Memo. To Mr. Scane at Edinr without being dated or signed.

A long letter full of news, written by a person with Jacobite leanings. Lord Lovat was taken prisoner by Lord Loudoun on 11 December, but he escaped from Inverness on the 20th, and immediately the Frazers marched to join the Prince under the Master of Lovat. When Lovat was eventually taken near Meoble on the southern shore of Loch Morar on 7 June 1746, the *Gentleman's Magazine* reported:

'He is 78 years of age, has a fine comely head to grace Temple Bar, and his body is so large, that I imagine the doors of the Tower must be altered to get him in. He can neither walk nor ride, and was brought here in a horse-litter, or rather a cage, as hardened as ever.'

He was executed on Tower Hill on 9 April 1747.

The Prince had received assurances of Spanish assistance when he was at Perth on the way to Edinburgh, and letters dated 1 August containing such promises, from the Kings of both France and Spain, were printed and circulated. They are said to have been brought over by Arbuthnot (see note to Letters 28 and 29), who brought over French arms and ammunition and accompanied them to Perth in October. The story mentioned in this letter, 'the money that came from Spain . . . came to Perth on the 19th,' does not, from contemporary accounts, appear to be true, as the only Spanish assistance which did arrive was confined to an occasional landing of privateers with money and stores, and a few officers who were taken with the 'Prince Charles' on 25 March 1746.

20 December was the Prince's birthday; he spent it fording the Esk and passing the night at the Buck Hotel, Annan. Judging by the celebrations described as taking place, it seems likely that this letter was written from Perth.

The Journal of the Marches of the Highland Army was printed by one James Grant, who joined the Prince before Prestonpans, procured a printing press on the way through Glasgow, and set it up at Bannockburn, where he printed both that journal and the *Bannockburn Journal*. There are copies of both these broadsheets in existence, and they are also printed in *The Lyon in Mourning*.

My Dear: It gives me great pleasure to hear ye are all in good health. I've seen one here who is a particular acquaintance of my

Bro. it is not long since he left him. He heard of him by those who came last from that place. His pupil was took ill at your S. house where he stayed some time, he was then very well. I doubt not but ye've heard that Ld L. [Lovat] was taken prisoner by Lowdon. He came with all his military pomp to take a lame man (which is a great shock to many). He says that if a hair of his fall to the Ground he will leave it on his clan to extirpate the names of Forbes, Brody, Monroe and MackLeod. He found out that he was to be sent to London in a ship, he has made his escape, it is said he is coming to Perth, where his Son came ten days ago with a great many Men and more coming. The money that came from Spain escorted by some hundreds of Glenronalds [Clanranalds] came to Perth on the 19th. Some say its 6000 and other say its not so much. The Arms are not come yet. The 20th was kept at Perth with great Solemnity. At noon the Cannon fired, the Bells rung, the Town was illuminate and at night there was a fine Ball for the Ladys. Most of the Highlanders is gone to Dunblain. Upon their going there, Lord Hume thought proper to leave Stirling. There is a great party gone to Fife commanded by Lord Cromarty, I believe to take up the contributions lay'd on there etc. It is lay'd on I hear according valued rent such as £100. Belches of Invermay has refused to pay. He has got a party of 60 on him, there is to be ten added every day I hear till its pay'd. People with you were foolish enough to think we are all low spirited in this country. Its far otherways, what satisfys those that are nearly concerned I dont hear. The Journal of the Marches of the Highland Army into England says that upon receiving Dispatches of importance at Derby a Council of War was called, where the P . . . . . was present, and it was resolved to return to Scotland. Some people conjecture it was from some great folks ascertaining of him being called by Par. That it may be so to be sure every true patriot prays to God, for it would prevent the shedding of much Blood on both sides. If it is not so, tis woe to these countrys. By Lord Drummond's declaration France and Spain is so strongly engaged it must be long ere it is determined. I intended to send the D and letter but I see by the papers its unnecessary. Some of the Life Guards that has come from the

P . . . . . says that he and all the army is in good health and top spirits. The Cannon was fired on the 28th for a Victory which Lord Lewis Gordon has had over Lord Loudon [*Skirmish of Inverurie* 23 December]. When Lord Lewis had sent of ye Express, many of the McLeods was killed and they had took about 100 of them Prisoners. The young and old Beard [Baird] and Monroe of Kilkern [Culcairn] run of in such haste they left their plads (the Government has fine Officers have they not). Lord Lewis was still on the pursuit. The Battle was at Old Meldrum on the 23d. There is further Accounts dayly expected. The Prisoners Officers is ordered from Perth on the Account of the bad usage their prisoners have met with, and some imprudent things that some of them has done whom you know which you would not believe it. But repeated informations has been given against them to the Governour [Lord Strathallan]. The places they are ordered to is Killamour [Killearn] Gleams [Glamis] and Couper [Coupar]. They make a great noise about it. Lord Drummond I hear is gone for Dunblain and the Cannon, so you may expect to hear of Stirling soon. Ld Albe[marle] is coming home, his men is ordered raise. The P . . . . . is now at Glasgow, sure enough his greatest Enemy must own that he has baffled all the Generals, and show'n himself the greatest one in Europe, and did people now think as they did of old, he well deserves to be a King. He has brought back his Army, with losing only 40 Men, dont believe a word you see in the News papers about them, tis all lyes. Pray make my Complements in the most obliging manner to all my friends. I wish ye all a happy new year. Adieu. Decemr 29th.

Memo. Intercepted letter sent me by Lieutent Knight relating to the Rebells.

LETTERS 90–106
(*See Foreword*)

The letters which follow are interesting because they throw some contemporary light on the workings of the Government spies in England as the Highland army advanced and then retreated.

Letter 93 contains an account of the Battle of Prestonpans, the death of Colonel Gardiner, and the ignominious flight of General Cope:

'Said the Berwickers unto Sir John,
"Oh, what's become of all your men?"
"I' faith," says he, "I dinna ken,
I left them 'a this morning." '

In Letter 98 there is a most colourful description of the entry of the Highland army into Lancaster, which took place actually on 25 November, though this letter is dated midnight on the 24th.

The 'Capt. Dudley Broadstreet' mentioned in Letter 102 was the author of a little book, reminiscent of the adventures of Baron Munchausen, entitled *The Life and Uncommon Adventures of Capt. Dudley Broadstreet, being the most Genuine and Extraordinary perhaps ever published*, printed in Dublin in 1755. Among other things Broadstreet writes that he was 'employ'd in Secret Services by the M . . . stry of G . . . t B . . . . . n in the Late Rebellion,' and that he was the cause of Prince Charles not marching direct on London from Derby. The 'Lieutenant Phillips' also mentioned in Letter 102 would seem to have proved his bona-fides, for he does not appear in the lists of prisoners.

Letter 106 brings the collection to a logical conclusion, with a short account of the Battle of Culloden and the total defeat of the Prince's army.

LETTER 90

Newcastle 10 Octr.

I saw a Gentleman this morning that came from Edinb: & he informs me that the Rebells are in their full March to Newcastle. I heard they were come to Berwick. Our Garrison is in good order. Our Gates and other Passages are walled up except four wch we have strong Guards at. We are daily taking up Spys that come from the North. We have 700 Dutch & 1000 English. Last Night 6000 English Troops landed at Shields from Flanders seven miles from Town which we expect tomorrow. Our troops are in good heart wishing every day to engage the Rebells who are strong about 12,000. Some desert daily whilst Numbers join them. The Pretender's Flag is the Crown & Coffin. The men he entertains he gives no Advance but one shilling promising five pounds when he is crowned. They strip people & rob them of all they have. We daily hear complaints of their ill usages. Edinb. Castle has entirely destroy'd the Town.

W. G.

LETTER 91

A copy of a letter from a Gentleman at Penrith to Thomas Shepherd Esqr at Kendal.

Penrith October 26.

From Dumfries we are advised that their Apprehensions there are considerably abated. They are determined to pay no Contribution unless there be no possibility of Security upon their Refusal but the Approach of his Majesties Forces has put them into high Spirits & a loyal Spirit manifests itself in a remarkable manner. Our former Accounts are now unquestionably confirmed that a considerable Body of well affected Clanns are actually under Arms commanded by Lord London [sic] By wch means the Rebells will be prevented from retreating wch (according to this Nights Accounts) they are anxiously endeavouring to secure. All our Informations (several of them are of undoubted Authority) agree that they are in the utmost Confusion and that even the Heads themselves are at variance. We are assured (whatever might be reported before) that they have had no Reinforcements but on the contrary daily Desertion, Perplexity & Confusion. I omit copying further since all is to the same purpose agreeable News to us. Not the least Hint of their moving South. I have rather diminish'd than magnified the information we have received this Evening.

Yours etc.

Manchester 28 Oct.

Last Night we had several Ltres from Newcastle wch all say the Rebels are intrenching themselves betwixt [?] near Dalkeith 4 miles on this side Edenb. Lord Viscount Kenmore & the Earl of Kilmarnock has joyn'd them [and] they give out they will there wait the King's Forces till they get near the Borders & then will make forced Marches for Carlisle & so come this way for London & give his Majesties Forces the slip. Genl. Oglethorpe & part of the Yorkshire Royal Hunters got to Newcastle last Friday. Genl. Wade & the Army will be there tomorrow. When he reaches Berwick he will be at least 20,000. The Yorkshire Hunters will make upwards of 1500 all well armed. 500 of them are Gents of the best Fortunes & each has 3 Servants or more all mounted on Tip top Hunters and are to fight undr the Command of Genl. Oglethorpe. An Action is expected betwn the Kings forces & the Rebells abt the 4th or 5th of Novembr or perhaps a day sooner.

G. R.

(Endorsed '26 & 28 Octr 1745 An Account of the Rebels.')

LETTER 93

Arrived hear last night the 4 of this instant November 1745.

One of his Majesty's Soldours of War who informes the publick that he was at the battle in Scotland and that he saw Colinol Garners Dragoons run away and that the Colinol Dismountd from his hors and pickt up a pike that Lay in the field and commanded at the head of the foote Till unfortunately he Lost his life and that General Cope was one of the first that Quit the field and he saw and stood 6 yards of Capt Rodgers when he hard him utter these words after his men had surrendered themselves prisoners of war thay asked him to surrender Likewise and his answer was that he was fighting for his king & Country and that he would sooner Loose his Life than surrender himself to any such Rebelous rascals as thay were and he killed 4 of the highlanders with his own hand when one of them came behind him with an ax and cut off his Lower Jaw and he fell to the ground and they knockt him on the head with the same weppon.

He says they have betwixt 2 & 3 Hundred of our men prisoners of war at Edinburgh and they youse them very unmercifull and tell them that thay shall not fair as thay Did at the battle of Preston the ridgment that this man belonged to are all taken prisoners So about 50 which made thear escapes to Berwick and this man is Going to London with Letters to the Government but for what account I nor thay know not which is all I have Learnt at present from

Yr Ever Dutiful & obedient servt J. J.

That this Captain rodgers was Quarter Master in his Grace the Duke of Montagues Hors when in Coventry Last and very well known by most of the inhabitants of the City and was afterwards made a Capt of foote.

(Endorsed '4 Novr 1745 Acct of our Defeat at Prestonpans.')

LETTER 94

Carlisle 9 Novr 1745.

Yours I rec'd & last night was brot in here a party of Light Horse & a prisoner belonging to the Rebels & this day he was sent to Genl. Wade. They are at Rawcliffe & this night encamp'd at a place called King's Moore 2 miles from this place. They were at Dumfries last night & took a few Horses.

T. H.

Sunday Eveng. 7 o'clock.

This minute an Express has confirm'd the above Account & says that Carlisle was determin'd to act on the defensive but it's apprehend'd in case the Rebels attack it as they have a great deal of heavy Artillery they can't hold out long.

(Endorsed '11 Novr 1745 the progress of the Rebels.')

LETTER 95

Preston 11 Novr.

This morning about 5 o'clock an Express arrived here from Lancastr wth a Copy of one from Carlisle wch you have at the foot of this. This Account has put the Town into the utmost Confusion imaginable. Its most people's opinion here the Rebels will reach our Town before the end of this week, I am etc.

J. M.

LETTER 96

Kendal Novr 17 1745
8 o'clock at Night.

Gentl.: I arrived at N. Castle Friday last and Delivd Col Grahams letter to Genl Wade who sent me word that he has nothing to send back to the Col. but his hble Service. Marshal Wade wth his army consisting of 16,000 men march'd at 10 o'clock from N. Castle Moor towd the Rebels & was to go the first Night [?] and the next to Hexham but co'd not learn the place they wo'd march to next they had employed so many horses to draw and carry their Baggage as I co'd not get one for a Messenger to bring a Letter here but was forced to ride most of last Night to get here soon. On Friday last the Town of Carlisle surrnd'd and shortly after the Castle. The Militia Officers & Govermen' were allowed to come out & go to their Respective homes upon Parole of Honour & not bearg arms agst the Pretendr. This indulgence was given them Upon Condition of 'em delivering up all their Arms & Horses which they accordingly did. I can at present give you no account of the Rebels but that they still continue at Carlisle. I think to stay a few days longer here & shall continue to give you as good Accounts as possible I am with great Regard,

Your hble servt
James Hasleden.

The Militia of Carlisle behaved exceeding gallantly untill the Town's People Capitulated without acquainting their military Friends. You may depend upon the Veracity of Marshall Wade, much as for an Eye Witness to it with Haste.

J. H.

Directed to the Mayor & Common Council of Liverpoole.
Pray excuse the inconsistency of my Writing being in great Haste.

Preston Monday 12 o'clock.

(Endorsed 'The Rebels at Carlisle 17 Novr 1745.')

LETTER 97

Lancaster Novr 23d 1745.

Gentn: An Express is arrived from Genl Wade wth an Acct that he is return'd to Newcastle finding it impracticable to Get his Artillery over the Moors. There are 800 Rebels within a few miles of this Town & are expected every moment. I assure you this is the only Express that has arriv'd since my last I have sat up these 2 Nights being in perpetual fear of their coming & my Horse is a mile out of Town I shall see some of you to-night & the best intelligence I can get out of 'em will Transmit you the first I have only time to write the above & I am Gentn

Your most humble
Servt
Jno Beynon.

N.B. The Rebels hold their Councels in the morning & march their vanguard to come in by 5 o'clock in the Eveng and all Lights to be put out at 9 o'clock & at Kendal 10 o'clock they march'd a Body of 2000 in & on Friday ye Pretender march'd into this Town, their nos are not known.

Preston Novr 24th 1745
at 12 o'clock at night.

Gentn : I sent you a ltr last night by Express wch I hope you have received—I was determin'd to see some of the Rebels & today at 12 o'Clock at noon came into Lancr a Quarter. Mastr. 6 Highlandrs. wth Blue Bonnets & white Cockades & 6 more Gentn wth Blue Coats & Scarlet Linings & 2 Servts for Attendance their Cockades are all white the Quarter Master lighted & went to the Town Hall & immediately issued out an order for the payment of the Excise & Customs, windo & Land Tax by 12 o'Clock on Monday upon Failure must take the Event & that order was declared in evry Street by the Belman. As soon as that was done a Body of 30 horse more came in & rec'ed Billets. The next Order issued Out was that all Butchers, Bakers, Farmers etc sho'd follow their Employment & bring in Provisions for P.C. R Troops upon pain of military Execution. Betwn 2 & 3 o'clock the Foot came in to the no. of 200 headed by Lord Elcho & instead of Drums they have Bagpipes to each Company. Then the Horse brot up the Rear. Lord Elcho gave me their King's Declaration for wch I thank'd him. His Quarters were at the same house I lodg'd at. By the nearest Calculation I co'd make, the Horse amounted to 120. The Foot as I observed before was 200, all Brave men, the Horse poorly mounted but in great Spirits & great plenty of money chiefly French Guineas & pay for what they have as they go on. The Speech given me by Lord Elcho in favour of a mock King I thought proper to serve in the same manner as a Hangman wo'd, that was to commit 'em to the Flames, being an Artful done thing by Kelly the Jesuit. Notwithstanding I disguised myself by wearing very bad Shoes tattered Stockings & hat slouched & every agreeable, a damn'd Papist had blown me as a Spy which item was given me by a Friend. I had guarded agst 'em by sending my horse out of Town & made my Escape in the night & came to Preston at 10 o'clock at night. As soon as the Troops were billetted a Guard was sett in all corners of the Town. From this place I shall go to Warrington where I shall continue my Intelligence by Express.

This will be the last post night at Preston. The Rebels will be here Monday night. As they advance all Intelligences will be at an End. I assure you I have taken all the pains I could to give you the earliest Intelligence. I belive I must buy a Horse for all the Common Horses are pressed for his Majesties Service & all Gentns Horses are sent out of every Town. Bed is almost a stranger to me these 3 nights. I shall avoid falling into Company wth the Rebels any more. Most of the Highlandrs have 2 pistols on each side of their Breast & a Musket slung over their Shoulders & a Broad Sword which they carry from the time they get up till they go to Bed.

Yours etc. John Beynon.

N.B. I had convers'd with 'em some time before I had idea to go. By an Express come this morning to the Merchts at Lancastr Genl. Wade is at Newcastle & will go to Halifax, Rochdale & so to Manchester—one o'clock morning—Another Express is arriv'd with an Account that 1200 came in at 9 o'clock at night.

(Endorsed '24 Novr 1745 The Rebels at Lancaster.')

LETTER 99

Knutsford Nov. 27 1745.
3 o'clock at noon.

Gentn: By a Messenger that left Lancaster yesterday 3 o'clock at noon who saw all the Rebel Army March from Lancaster & says they are not 8000 men. The Pretender march'd at the head of 4 or 5000 horse & Foot. The Duke of Perth's Coach & Six follows with his lady and two or more Young Ladies & Old Glenbucket. The Pretender's Mistress follows in a Chair drawn by two horses & Several Young Ladies on horseback. It is imagin'd they will fix their Standard on Delamoor Forest or else some where near Manchester. Great numbers of the Country Gentn are Fled here that live about Preston so that I am sure of the best Intelligence here. They behave very peaceably upon the road & likewise in their Quarters. They set at liberty all the Debtors that were at Lancaster Castle All the Felons and them for Murder were committed to the care of the Gaoler.

I am etc.

Jno Beynon.

N.B. The advanced Guard of the Rebels are got to Chorley.

(Endorsed '27 Novr 1745 The Rebels at Chorley etc.')

LETTER 100

Knutsford Novr 29 1745.

Gentn : The Rebels came to Manchester this morning they entered the Town & a mob rose shouted 'em & enlisted to the number of 50 & amongst 'em 2 parsons they had white Cockades put into their hats immediatly & went abt the Town to enlist others. The pretendr is expected there this afternoon. It's greatly feared that Numbers of the Manufactuary will join 'em. This is the needful at present.

From yours etc.

J. Beynon.

(Endorsed '29 Nov. 1745 The Rebels at Manchester.')

LETTER 101

Holmes Chapple 1st Decr 1745.

Gentn : I left Knutsford last night & the Rebels came in there today abt 12 o'clock. It is the opinion of Col Graham & Col Gordon that they will march for Shrewsbury in Order to avoid Duke William's Army if they shod do so & get into Wales. It may be of bad Consequence they have raised a great Numbr of Recruits at Manchestr & amongst the Gentn Volunteers Mr Peter Moss is enlisted. A party of the Duke of Kingston's horse who were ordd to watch the motions of the Rebels it's greatly feared have fell into the hands of the Rebels betwn Knutsford & Altringham today they fell down some trees & made good the part of the Bridge thrown down in a few hours By wch means they will be able to get all their Artillery over the Mersey. At Manchester they Ordrd the Bells to ring & made Bonfires in sevl parts of the town & occasioned all the windows to be illuminated the Night the Pretendr came to Town

I am Sir etc.

John Beynon.

(Endorsed 'i Decr 1745 The Rebels at Knutsford.')

LETTER 102

To his Grace the Duke of Newcastle.

May it please your grace

Mr Mayor and the Magistrates have stopped a person here, who calls himself Lieut Wm. Phillips of Genl Read's Regiments. He is a man of the first Size in a Military Garb; He travelled from Dunstable to this place with Capt Dudley Broadstreet, who informs us that he was pretty Curious in his Enquiries & in making his observations Upon the Road, & let slip some disaffected Expressions.

Upon Searching him we have found the enclosed papers, which we have not disclosed, but thought proper to hasten them to your Grace, & as he discovers great Backwardness & reluctance to be examined, the Magistrates have resolved to detain him, till they shall know your Grace's pleasure concerning him.

I am,

my Lord

Your Graces must obedient &

most humble Servant

J. B. Town Clerk.

Capt Broadstreet writes to your Grace by this Express.
The Prisoner owns he has been in company at a Shooting with the Pretender's 2 Sons.
Capt. Phillip's pocket Book not open'd.
Wedn 4 Decr 1745 past 3 afternoon.

LETTER 103

Kendall 25 Dec 1745.

We hear they are Bombarding Carlisle & the Rebels make a strong fire from the Walls. They have sent Twice to the Duke for a Capitulation, but the Duke returned Answer he wou'd give no Quarter this is what came from Carlisle yesterday.

Jn Wilson.

past 7 o'clock at Night.

The Cannon from Whitehaven came yesterday to Carlisle. The Batteries were erecting & would play last Night or to-day; they had hanged 4 of the Rebels that Morning.

Jnº Wilson.

P.S. The Messenger says that there are 3000 of the Rebels in Carlisle, 100 Prisoners at Penrith & 72 at Appleby & that Ld Loudoun joined by pt of General Wades men has stopt & demolish'd those that had got into Scotland. This I send as report but he says his fact and further Genl Wade with The Artillery & 4000 Men has join'd the Duke.*

* The above is a Copy of the Acct come this Day & tho' some particulars in it are not true yet it's certain the Rebels are in Carlisle to the Number of 3000, also of the Cannon from Carlisle, tho' its said the Pretender with most of the Chiefs are got off in Boats & gon for Scotland.

LETTER 104

Preston 27 Dec 1745.

Dr Joe: I rote to you last Post which I hope rec'd since which we have rec'd no Material Accounts out of the North except by Genl Oglethorps Servt who came here this Evening he tells me he left Carlisle last night that the Duke had rec'd the heavy Cannon from Whitehaven & that they were raising Batteries & making Preparations to play upon the City which I hope they have effected 'ere this. That St George's Dragoons & a party of Wades Horse had took 30 Cartload of Baggage belonging to the Rebels, that it was generally believed from the Number of the Rebels taken Prisoners, those drown'd in the River Esk & the party of Horse which had passed over the Bridge East of Carlise, that there were abt 2000 in the City. Its not doubted but those which have made their Escape from Carlisle will meet with their Desert as the Duke has sent a Detachment after them & have Forces North of them.

LETTER 105

Friday 3 Jany 1745.

This day a Messenger dispatched by the Duke came thro' here, acquainting us that the Rebels in Carlisle surrenderd on Thursday last the 31 decr and are all now prisoners in the Church there are about 500 of them in number.

(Endorsed '25 & 27 Decr & 3d Jan: 1745 The Duke's Investing Carlisle & the Surrender.')

LETTER 106

Last night came here Two Expresses to Lord Warrington brought an Account they had killed & took prisoners 4000 of the Rebels— that the Duke of Perth was amongst the slain, the Pretender wounded in the Knee & fled into the Highlands & a party was gone after him. Most of their Chiefs are either killed or taken prisoners but their names I've quite forgot. Everybody believes it true. There's great Rejoicing everywhere.

. . . . Altringham near Ld Warrington's.

28 April 1746.

29 April. This came to Mrs. Morris of Ridgley & was forwarded to Mr. Jones the Glover of Birmingham this day.

(Endorsed '28 Apr 1746 Acct of the Rebels Defeat at Culloden.')

A SHORT BIBLIOGRAPHY

Bell, Robert F. (Ed.). *Memorials of John Murray of Broughton.* Scottish History Society. (Edinburgh, 1898.)

Blaikie, Walter B. *Itinerary of Prince Charles Edward Stuart.* Scottish History Society. (Edinburgh, 1797.)

—— (Ed.). *Origins of the Forty-Five.* Scottish History Society. (Edinburgh, 1916.)

Chambers, Robert. *History of the Rebellion in 1745.* (Edinburgh, 1869.)

Forbes, J. Macbeth. *Jacobite Gleanings.* (Edinburgh, 1903.)

Forbes, Bishop Robert. *The Lyon in Mourning.* Ed. Henry Paton. Scottish History Society. 3 vols. (Edinburgh, 1895-6.)

Gentleman's Magazine, 1744-7.

Lang, Andrew. *Prince Charles Edward Stuart.* (London, 1900.)

—— *Pickle the Spy.* (London, 1897.)

—— *Companions of Pickle.* (London, 1898.)

London Gazette, 1745-6.

London Magazine, 1744-7.

Nicholas, Donald. *The Young Adventurer.* (London, 1949.)

Oliphant, T. L. Kingston. *The Jacobite Lairds of Gask.* Grampian Club. (London, 1879.)

Rosebery, Earl of (Ed.). *A List of Persons concerned in the Rebellion.* Scottish History Society. (Edinburgh, 1890.)

Seton, Sir Bruce Gordon, and Arnot, J. G. (Eds.). *Prisoners of the Forty-Five.* Scottish History Society. 3 vols. (Edinburgh, 1928-9.)

Seton, Sir Bruce Gordon, Bt. (Ed.) *Orderly Book of Lord Ogilvy's Regiment.* (Manchester, 1923.)

Tayler, Alistair and Henrietta. *Jacobites of Aberdeenshire and Banffshire in the '45.* (Aberdeen, 1928.)

INDEX

Abernethy, Alexander, 38, 39
Abernethy, Helen, 39
Adie, William, 37
Albemarle, Lord, 36
Almond, Lady Logie, 28, 43
Anderson, D., 89
Anderson, James, 69
Arbuthnot, James Carnegy, 53, 55, 56, 133
Arbuthnott, James, 77
Ardshiel, Lord, 22
Atholl, Duke of, 52, 100, 101, 102
Auchenleck, Andrew, 96, 97
Auchterlony, John, 119

Baird, William, 104
Bannerman, Sir John, 65
Barclay, Miss, 48
Belches, John, 23, 36
Berwick, 36, 100, 101, 129, 136
Beynon, John, 143, 144, 145
Borradale, 17
Brand, Alexander, 76
Breadalbane, 100
Broadstreet, Captain Dudley, 136, 145
Brown, Laurence, 32
Burnett, James, 85

Cameron, Dr. Archibald, 30
Cameron, Donald, of Lochiel, 30
Cameron, Duncan, 49
Camerons, 100
Carlisle, 108, 109, 123, 138, 139, 140, 141
Carmichael, 103, 104
Clanranald, Lord, 22
Clifton, 33
Cope, Sir John, 17, 18, 19, 138
Crawford, Charles, 51
Crawford, James, 50

Cromartie, Lord, 74, 75, 100, 122, 126, 134
Cruikshank, William, 63
Culloden, 22, 30, 31, 42, 74, 95, 109, 121, 136, 147
Cumberland, Duke of, 22, 35
Cumine, Charles, 95, 96
Cumming, James, 28
Cumming, Mrs., 111

Dalkeith, 24
DeBoyer, Jean Baptiste, 22
Demand on Glasgow, 48
D'Eguilles, Marquise, 22
Derby, retreat from, 22, 53, 113
Dotte, Mrs. Anne, 26
Douglas, Lord, 100
Douglas, William, 61, 91
Drummond, Lady Frances, 128
Drummond, James, 18
Drummond, Lord John, 53, 54, 58, 59, 126, 134
Drummond, Mrs., 27
Duff, Miss Harriet, 105
Duguid, Patrick, 74, 100
Dunbar, John, 98
Dundonald, Lady, 37

Eglinton, Lord, 20, 21
Elcho, Lord, 22, 100
Elibank, Lord, 25
Elibank plot, 25
Elphinston, 53
Erskine, Alexander (Earl of Kelly), 42
Erskine, Captain John, 54, 56, 126

Farquharson, Francis, 73
Farquharson, James, 73
Fauld, James, 127, 129
Fergusly, Lady, 24

Ferguson, James, of Pitfour, 24
Ferriers, David, 54, 56
Ferriers, Captain, 126
Fleming, David, 32
Forbes, Alexander, 78, 79
Forbes, Thomas, 78
Forbes, Lord President, 17, 100
Forbes, Mrs., 94
Fort William, 18
Fotheringham, David, 49
Fourdon, 23
Frazer, Mrs., 20
Frazer, Anne, 40
Frazer, Betty, 40
Frazer of Gortleg, 17

Galloway, Earl of, 94, 95
Galloway, Lord, 100
Gardiner's Dragoons, 17
Gibbon, William, 79, 80, 81
Glascoe, Major Nicholas, 126
Glenbucket, Lord, 22
Glencoe, Lord, 22
Glenfinnan, 17
Glendyle, Lord, 100
Glenshiel, 31
Goold, Thomas, 54
Gordon, Amy, 85, 86, 87
Gordon, Charles, 29, 73
Gordon, George, 82
Gordon, Henrietta, Duchess, 33, 34, 35
Gordon, Lady Janet, 61, 62, 63, 64
Gordon, Lady Jean, 33, 41, 42, 43, 84
Gordon, John, of Avochie, 66
Gordon, John, of Glenbucket, 74, 100
Gordon, Sir John, of Park, 101
Gordon, Lord Lewis, 22, 33, 62, 66, 67, 106, 119, 135
Gordon, Sir William, 33, 61
Grant, Captain, 24
Grant, James, 133
Grant, Laird of, 18
Grant, Ludovick, 17

Hamilton, John, 87, 88
Hamley, General, 109
Hardy, Captain Alexander, 100, 101

Hasleden, James, 140
Hawley, General, 59
Hay, James, 68
Hay, Lord, of Ramas, 101
Hay, Sir Thomas, 101
Hazard, 54 124, 125, 126
Hepburn, Katherine, 107, 108
Heres, Mrs., 20
Hill, Captain, 124, 125, 126
Holyroodhouse, 21, 32
Home, Sir William, 23

Inchmartin, Laird of, 91, 103
Innes, George, 75
Innes, Colonel James, 113, 114
Innes, John, 92
Inverlochy, Lord, 101
Inverness, 22, 29

Johnston, William, 88

Kelly, Lord, 100, 101
Kenmore, Lord Viscount, 138
Keppach, Lord Lochiel, 22
Kilmarnock, Lord, 59, 100, 138
Knight, Lieutenant, 135

Leslie, Mrs., 28
Leslie, William, 114
Letham, Patrick, 82
Ligonier, Colonel, 129
Linlithgow, Lord James, 59
Lochgarry, Lord, 22
Lochiel, Lord, 19, 100
Lockhart, George, 22, 23, 27, 100
Longmoor, Andrew, 104
Loudoun, Lord, 24, 119, 120, 133, 135, 137
Lovat, Lord Simon, 17, 18, 133
Lyon, Cecilia (Mrs.), 124
Lyon, George, 127
Lyon, Rev. Robert, 123

MacDonald, General, 18
MacDonald, Sir Alexander, 21, 57, 65, 72, 97, 100
MacDonald, Flora, 21
MacDonald of Tendrish, 17

MacDonald, Sir John, 17, 22
MacDonald, Lady Margaret, 21
McGrigors, 1, 100
McIntoshes, 121
McIntyre, Donald, 29, 30, 31
McKay, Robert, 25
MacKenzie, George, 74
McKinnins, 100
Mackintosh, Lady Anne, 57, 121
McLauchlan, Dougald, 46, 100
McLeods, 100
McPherson, Cluny, 21, 100
McPherson, Kenneth, 30
M'Vicar, 23
Manifesto, 18
Marshal, Lord, 58
Menzies, William, 79
Mill, Captain, 127
Milne, Janett, 28
Moir, James, 74
Moir, William, 85, 86
Montague, Duke of, 139
Montrose, 22, 54, 63, 65, 66, 124, 125,
126, 127, 129
Morgan, David, 113
Morton, Lord Douglas, 63
Mudie, George, 127
Muire, Miss, 47
Munro of Culcairn, 24
Murray, Lord John, of Broughton,
22, 100
Murray, Lord George, 22, 72, 101,
109
Murray, 'Mr. Evidence', 42
Murray, Patrick, 97
Murray, William (Duke of Atholl),
31

Nairn, Lord, 22
Newcastle, 35, 129, 136
Newcastle, Duke of, 25, 27
Newtown of Rockcliff, 52
Nisbet, Miss Willy, 132

Ogilvie, Lady, 57
Ogilvie, Lady Betty, 104
Ogilvie, Lady Margaret, 25
Ogilvie, Lord, 22, 55, 76, 100

Ogilvy, William, 84
Oglethorpe, General, 138
Oliphant, Laurence, 44, 45
Ormond, Duke of, 58
O'Sullivan, Lord, 22

Paterson, Mrs., 76
Pearson, Captain Gray, 127
Perth, Duke of, 18, 22, 33, 52, 100,
101, 102, 143
Pitfour, 26
Pitsligo, Lord, 22, 100
Prestonpans, Battle of, 19, 21, 28, 42,
48, 89, 121, 133, 136, 139

Reid, John, 21
Reynolds, Luke, 59
Riddock, Thomas, 114
Robertson, Alexander, 73, 117, 122
Robertson, Rev. William, 19
Rodgers, Captain, 138
Ross, Malcolm, 121
Ross, Robert, 21
Royal Scots, 17
Russell, David, 51

Sangster, James, 28
Savoy Chapel, 30
Scane, Mr., 132
Scott, Captain, 17
Scott, John, 98
Scott, William, 48, 49
Scraw, Miss Jeany, 128
Seton, Peter, 101, 102
Sharp, Miss Margaret, 60
Sharp, Mrs. Peggy, 91
Shepherd, Thomas, 137
Sheridan, Lord, 22
Shields, 136
Smith, Alexander, 114, 115, 116
Smith, William, 18
Stewarts, 100
Stone, William, 41
Stonehaven, 22, 54, 65, 66, 116, 117,
127
Strathallan, Lord, 53, 91
Strichen, Lord, 111, 112, 113
Stuart, Lady Frances, 57

151

Stuart, Lady Mary, 40
Stuart, George, 71
Stuart, John, 29

Thomson, John, 126
Tomson, Helen, 77
Trotter, Thomas, 38
Tullibardine, Marquis of, 31
Turner, John, 131

Turner, Margaret (née Farquharson), 99, 100, 102, 103, 130

Wade, Marshal, 35, 52, 100, 101, 109, 113, 129, 138, 140, 141
Wallace, Captain, 127
Warrington, Lord, 147
Watson, John, 77
Wilson, John, 146
Wilson, Mrs. Jennett, 20